SURVIVING TERROR

TRUE TEEN STORIES FROM AROUND THE WORLD

True Teen Stories from

AFGHANISTAN AND PAKISTAN

Surviving the Taliban

Cassandra Schumacher

Cavendish
Square

New York

Published in 2019 by Cavendish Square Publishing, LLC
243 5th Avenue, Suite 136, New York, NY 10016

Library of Congress Cataloging-in-Publication Data

Names: Schumacher, Cassandra, author.
Title: True teen stories from Afghanistan and Pakistan : surviving the
Taliban / Cassandra Schumacher.
Description: First edition. | New York, NY : Cavendish Square Publishing,
LLC, 2019. | Series: Surviving terror: true teen stories from around the
world | Includes bibliographical references and index.
Identifiers: LCCN 2017061194 (print) | LCCN 2018004367 (ebook) |
ISBN 9781502635518 (eBook) | ISBN 9781502635501 (library bound) |
ISBN 9781502635525(pbk.)
Subjects: LCSH: Taliban--Juvenile literature. |
Afghanistan--History--2001---Juvenile literature. |
Pakistan--History--21st century--Juvenile literature. | Child
soldiers--Afghanistan--History--21st century--Juvenile literature. | Child
soldiers--Pakistan--History--21st century--Juvenile literature. | Teenage
soldiers--Afghanistan--History--21st century--Juvenile literature. |
Teenage soldiers--Pakistan--History--21st century--Juvenile literature. |
Girls--Afghanistan--History--21st century--Juvenile literature. |
Girls--Pakistan--History--21st century--Juvenile literature. |
Terrorism--Afghanistan--History--21st century--Juvenile literature. |
Terrorism--Pakistan--History--21st century--Juvenile literature.
Classification: LCC DS371.3 (ebook) | LCC DS371.3 .S38 2019 (print) | DDC
958.104/7092535--dc23
LC record available at https://lccn.loc.gov/2017061194

Editorial Director: David McNamara
Editor: Caitlyn Miller
Copy Editor: Rebecca Rohan
Associate Art Director: Amy Greenan
Designer: Christina Shults
Production Coordinator: Karol Szymczuk
Photo Research: J8 Media

The photographs in this book are used by permission and through the courtesy of:
Cover, Mark Pearson/Alamy Stock Photo; pp. 4, 62 Knut Müller/ullstein bild/Getty Images; p. 8
Renee's illustrations/Shutterstock.com; p. 13 Pictures From History/Newscom; p. 17 United States
Department of State/File: U.S. Department of State official seal.svg/Wikimedia Commons/Public
Domain; p. 26 Bettmann/Getty Images; p. 34 Tass/Getty Images; p. 39 Emmanuel Dunand/AFP/
Getty Images; pp. 43, 74 Saeed Khan/AFP/Getty Images; p. 45 Micheline Pelletier/Sygma/Getty
Images; p. 46 Oleg Nikishin/Getty Images; p. 51 AP Photo/Rafiq Maqbool; p. 55 Farshad Usyan/
AFP/Getty Images; p. 56 José Nicolas/Sygma/Getty Images; p. 64 Khan Raziq/Anadolu Agency/
Getty Images; p.70 Patrick Piel/Gamma-Rapho/Getty Images; p. 78 Michael Kovac/FilmMagic/
Getty Images; p. 86 Mandel Ngan/AFP/Getty Images; p. 92 U.S. Marines/ISAF Headquarters Public
Affairs Office/File: Opium poppies in Helmand -a.jpg/Wikimedia Commons/Public Domain.

Printed in the United States of America

CONTENTS

1 The Taliban in Afghanistan
and Pakistan 5

2 A Closer Look at the Rise
of the Taliban 27

3 Young Recruits 47

4 The Casualties of the Taliban:
Living with Terror 65

5 Solving Terror 87

Chronology 100

Glossary 101

Further Information 103

Bibliography 105

Index 110

About the Author 112

This photograph of an armed member of the Taliban in Wana, Pakistan, was taken in 2008.

CHAPTER ONE

THE TALIBAN IN AFGHANISTAN AND PAKISTAN

Almost everyone born in the last fifty years in the Western world has heard the word "Taliban," a terrorist organization whose attacks have shaped countries around the world. Words like "bombing" and "war" often follow. In Afghanistan and Pakistan, these terms are more than faraway concepts; in those countries, they are a way of life.

For years, under the Taliban in Afghanistan and Pakistan, women were shut in. During the late 1980s, refugee camps in Pakistan that housed Afghan refugees were the roots of the Taliban. The ideology and extreme fundamentalism characteristic of the Taliban began to form in these camps and would spread in both countries over the coming years.

Some people who were displaced by war found comfort in the extremist law and sharia law that would become Taliban ideology. These ideas spread to Afghanistan, and the Afghan Taliban began to form and draw strength. These militants took control in Afghanistan in 1996. Though the Pakistani Taliban, once known as the Tehrik-i-Taliban, and the Taliban in Afghanistan are two different groups, because of their shared origins in Afghan refugee camps in Pakistan, their ideology is much the same.

Under the Taliban in both countries, men were forced to grow full beards. Children could not fly kites or dance or play music. Even weddings were performed without music. Movies did not play in theaters, and televisions were banned. Over the radio, messages from an unseen mullah played, speaking of the value of sharia law. Girls stopped going to school and had to be dressed from the tops of their heads to the tips of their toes to step outside—and even then, they needed a chaperone. A person could be beaten in the street for not following the strict rules laid out by the Taliban. Yet it was also under the Taliban in Afghanistan that people saw the end to a ravaging civil war.

The streets and cities were mangled by war, left in rubble by bombings and infighting. Men patrolled the cities and rural areas with massive guns, but there was the illusion of peace for the first time in years in Afghanistan. The quiet of the streets was in stark contrast to the roar of bombs heard in the cities for so long. People no longer woke up in the mornings to call on family to see if everyone had survived the night. Whole families were no longer wiped out in bombing raids. Men with guns maintained the peace of the streets for the first time in years, but such quiet could not last for long. Soon Westerners would come, bringing war to Afghanistan yet again.

With the arrival of Western allies, the strict and fundamental Islamic reign of the Taliban would end in Afghanistan, but their presence would always loom. The values that the Taliban put in place remained, leaving stringent expectations for society, behavior, and people's ways of life. People were still deeply devout, yet men began to shave their beards and some women took off their burkas. Access to previously limited commodities returned with Western influence. Internet access and other technology started popping up throughout the country. Access to hospitals and schools for girls showed a changing nation. Democracy came with Western intervention. However, the budding democratic government did not have the strength to stand without support from other nations and NATO. The new government could not hold the country without military allies, and though the Taliban's reign ended in 2001, they were not eradicated. It was during this time that

The Afghanistan-Pakistan border is a point for Taliban ideology and militants to cross between the two countries.

their Pakistani counterparts began to rise in the tribal lands of Pakistan.

Today, the Taliban still occupies large portions of Afghanistan and is found in the tribal lands of Pakistan. Followers have strongholds across the country in Afghanistan, and they continue to grow and regain power, spreading their defined and extremely stringent form of Islamic law in both countries. They seek to regain the control of their respective nations. They are strong, and they are persistent. The Taliban will not willingly surrender Afghanistan or Pakistan to progressive ideals. Members of the Taliban hide in the hills and also walk through the streets in some parts of each country. Even as fear of terror and terrorists grows on the world stage, the two Taliban groups continue to regain power.

Afghanistan

Home to more than thirty-four million people, Afghanistan is located in a landlocked region split by the Hindu Kush mountains. Like other nations in the Middle East, Afghanistan is part of the continent of Asia, located close to where the continent connects with Africa. The nation is situated between the main landmasses of Asia and Africa.

The Hindu Kush mountains cover a majority of the country. It is a hilly and mountainous land with the tallest peak, Mount Tirich Mir, near the border of Afghanistan and Pakistan. The mountains make the climate arid and dry. The summers are hot, and the winters are cold. Afghanistan is a rugged country with many untapped resources.

More than 99 percent of the nation's population is Muslim. Most of the population are Sunni Muslims, but there is a small sect of Shia Muslims. There is a history of ethnic conflict that has impacted the region, and faith is a very important part of life in Afghanistan.

Pakistan

Pakistan is an ecologically diverse country. There are foothills, mountains, plateaus, and plains. There is even a fertile river valley along the Indus River that contrasts the desert areas that can also be found in the country.

It is a nation plagued by political instability. Though legally the government is supposed to be independent of religion, a driving force behind the election of candidates is their allegiance to Sunni Muslim ideology.

The nation achieved independence from India in 1947 but divided again in 1971 in a civil war that resulted in the formation of Bangladesh. There have been a series of coups since then. The current government consists of a president and a two-house parliament. The Federally Administered Tribal Areas (FATA) have a history of Taliban support and occupation. These lands are found mostly around the border between Afghanistan and Pakistan. Insurgents have been known to cross the border both ways, seeking sanctuary and support.

Afghanistan Before the Taliban

There was a far more progressive lifestyle with greater access to education for women in the 1960s in Afghanistan. At that time, Afghanistan's very progressive king advocated for greater liberties and freedoms, but he was met with some resistance. Photos provided by an American doctor from a visit to Kabul at this time show women studying at universities in knee-length skirts. Modern cars are visible, and the images are markedly different than the pictures painted of Afghanistan after the Taliban. The liberal king's progressive aims did not coincide with those of the nation's deeply conservative Muslim population. It was not hard to imagine that with such differences in perspective, the Afghani political structure was vulnerable and would fall in the coming decades.

The monarchy leading the nation during the 1970s did not have a firm grip, and a democratic coup left the country even less protected from outsiders. A military coup and the rise of a communist party created an uncertain political climate. At the tail end of the Cold War conflict, communist Soviets arrived in Afghanistan in 1979 to ensure communism took hold. They brought horror and war to the country. What followed was a violent and terrible time. The Soviets kept control by killing off those who protested their power and leadership. The social policies that the Soviets put in place led to resistance from the populace because those policies did not correspond with Muslim beliefs. Furthermore, the laws that were passed made life more challenging for the poor in the country. People rose up against the Soviets. Conflict with the Soviets included ethnic uprisings, which were stopped with violence like torture and execution, arrests, and bombings of the Afghani people. Amnesty International estimates that during this horrible time one million people died, and of that one million, eight thousand were executed.

In true Cold War tradition, the United States followed Soviet action in Afghanistan by encouraging and funding resistance efforts against Soviet control. The United States did so by backing Afghani freedom fighters known as mujahideen. The fighting intensified with US support, and the Afghani resistance's guerrilla tactics made them hard for Soviet soldiers to catch and stamp out. The Soviets tried to regain control by bombing rural areas to eliminate the resistance, but instead these actions fed Afghani anger and intensified the mujahideen's desire to fight. Bombings only added to the public support behind the resistance. This, paired with military air power provided by the United States, helped the mujahideen gain the upper hand. By the late 1980s, the Soviets were losing their hold on Afghanistan just as they were losing strength worldwide. In 1989, the Soviets finally withdrew but left the country in turmoil. A power vortex opened up, leaving the country vulnerable yet again. This power vacuum was even more dangerous than the one after the monarchy fell. The warlords of Afghanistan began their fight for power.

MULLAH OMAR

Experts believe Mullah Mohammed Omar looks like this computer-generated composite.

Mullah Mohammad Omar was the spiritual leader of the Taliban. Though the exact date of his birth is unknown, it is assumed to be either 1959 or 1960. He passionately studied Islam as a young man. Omar was injured fighting as a mujahideen against the Soviets and the communist regime that was in place after they left. These injuries included the loss of an eye.

There are different stories about why Omar was chosen to lead the Taliban, but the general consensus of Taliban members is he was either chosen by God or that he earned the right when he rescued two abducted teenage girls. The girls were said to have been taken and abused in a military camp in 1994. This second story made him into a hero of the people.

There was a thick shroud of secrecy around Mullah Omar. Little information can be confirmed about him. What is known is that the ranks of the Taliban swelled under Omar's guidance. He called for and enforced sharia law and gradually took control of Afghanistan. Omar was ousted as leader of the country when American forces invaded Afghanistan, but he continued to lead the Taliban from hiding. Though the Taliban concealed his death until 2015, it is believed that Mullah Omar most likely died in April 2013.

The Taliban

The Soviet retreat from Afghanistan led to massive amounts of infighting. Many different people wanted control of the country, and their efforts left the country in chaos. Civil war broke out among warlords, who were power hungry and seeking control. In some ways, it seemed that the country was worse off than it had begun. A fundamentalist Islamic group, the Taliban, offered a chance at normalcy to people who desperately sought calm. Some people were willing to trade oppression for an end to civil war. The Taliban was, in many ways, a means to peace, even if the group ruled through terror.

Once they rose to power, the Taliban became known as an extremist, fundamentalist Islamic group. Members of the Taliban view themselves as enlightened and their actions within Afghanistan as a tribute to God. Taliban translates to "student," and many members see themselves as religious scholars seeking the most holy way of life. It is through such studies of the Quran, the Muslim holy book, that the Taliban began to push for sharia law. They view sharia law as the most effective and religiously driven method of ruling. Sharia law is based on the Quran and the hadith—the words of the prophet Mohammed. The punishments for crimes under sharia law are swift and brutal.

Some of these include execution, stoning, lashings, or limb amputation. Such violence was also the tool the Taliban used to maintain control. According to the Taliban, sharia law is God's preferred way of life. The Taliban's application of sharia law, however, was singular. It, to this day, is counted as one of the strictest, least forgiving implementations of sharia law in the Islamic world.

Women's rights also declined steeply under the Taliban regime. Women were not granted access to education or even the outside world. A woman was allowed to leave her home only with a male family member as an escort. Girls' schools were closed, and women were expected to wear full burkas in public. Though many Muslim women choose to wear a veil or head covering known as a hijab that covers the hair and sometimes the neck, a full burka is designed to cover the entire body including the face and eyes. A small mesh or lace window covers a woman's eyes so that she may see out, but no one can see in. Some women do choose to wear full burkas as an expression of their faith, but the Taliban mandated that all women, regardless of preference, were to be fully covered in public. Limited access to technology and media also helped the Taliban control the spread of their messages and restrict access to the outside world. Music and media were not considered holy, and religious messages filled the radio waves once they both were banned.

THE BUREAU OF COUNTERTERRORISM AND COUNTERING VIOLENT EXTREMISM

The United States has an antiterrorism organization known as the Bureau of Counterterrorism that became the Bureau of Counterterrorism and Countering Violent Extremism in 2016. A majority of the work done by the bureau focuses on neutralizing international threats and defeating terrorism locally, as well as globally. With the rise in global attacks since the 1990s and 2000s, terrorism has been categorized as one of the greatest threats to national security. Fear of terror organizations like al-Qaeda, the Taliban, and ISIS has led to increased security measures and greater attention to the threats rising in international politics. The goal of the Bureau of Counterterrorism and Countering Violent Extremism is to help combat terrorist organizations and protect the United States. The bureau pays special attention to the unique and violent threat that terrorist organizations present. The goal is to minimize the effects of terror groups on the United States as a nation as well as the world as a whole.

This fits within the global effort to counter terrorism. In 2011, the Global Counterterrorism Forum (GCTF) was founded. The forum consists of twenty-nine nations working together on

The US Department of State works to combat national and global terror threats.

methods to fight terrorism as it exists in the twenty-first century. The US Department of State describes the organization as having the goal to "identify urgent needs, devise solutions, and mobilize resources for additional counterterrorism challenges." The GCTF hopes to build up support for counterterrorism measures and to ensure the world's safety against terrorist organizations. The aim of both the Bureau of Counterterrorism and Countering Violent Extremism and the GCTF is safeguarding people from the violence of extremist groups.

Power was concentrated in the hands of a few people. The main leader was Mullah Mohammad Omar until 2015, when his death was announced. Other leaders included Mullah Akhtar Mohammad Mansour and Mawlawi Haibatullah Akhundzada. Mansour was killed in an air strike in 2016 after his election in 2015. Akhundzada is the current leader, elected after Mansour's death. The leaders of the Taliban tend to be shrouded in secrecy. Information surrounding them and their lives is minimal. Their locations are kept secret to protect them from the Afghan military and its allies. What is known is that the leader is often a deeply religious man who expresses the ideas of the Taliban and truly embraces sharia law. While commanding the Taliban, the leader bears the title "amīr al-mu'minīn," which means "commander of the faithful."

The Pakistani Taliban

The Pakistani Taliban's origin story coincides with that of the Afghan Taliban. While the Taliban was gaining strength in Afghanistan, Pakistani sympathizers were organizing and providing assistance over the border. It is interesting that Pakistan was one of only three nations that recognized the Taliban as the leaders of Afghanistan when they took the capital in 1996. (The other two were Saudi Arabia and the United Arab Emirates.) Especially in the lands near the Pakistan-Afghanistan border, support groups began to flourish. However, it was not until 2001 to 2002 that they saw enormous growth. The Pakistani Taliban was not recognized as an independent terror organization until the period between 2002 and 2004; prior to that time period, they were simply considered Afghan Taliban sympathizers.

Unlike the Taliban in Afghanistan, the Pakistani Taliban has never gained control of their nation. Most of the Pakistani Taliban's holdings are near the border of the two countries, and they have never held the majority of Pakistan's land like the Taliban did in Afghanistan. They are also more divided than the Afghan Taliban.

The Pakistani Taliban is equally violent, but their power is less centralized. In many ways, the Pakistani Taliban is more like a collection of factions. Independent militias that are loosely unified make up the terror group. The whole is the sum of its parts, rather than having one tightly unified organization under an individual leader as in Afghanistan.

The funding for the Pakistani Taliban is also different. They receive funds from the opium trade of the Afghan Taliban, but they are also more of a grassroots-funded organization. They receive money and donations from people living in the territories they hold. The Pakistani Taliban also farms tobacco, illegally logs forests, and mines marble and emeralds, but most of their funds are extorted or stolen from

Pakistani citizens. They even rob banks and kidnap people in order to make money through ransoms. Afghanistan's Taliban has a much more focused stream of revenue.

Funding the Taliban

Smuggling finances the Afghan Taliban. The Taliban moves arms, cigarettes, and, most importantly, narcotics. They are a major source of heroin, as well as hashish. In fact, the Taliban controls nearly 90 percent of the opium trade in the world. The group also owns some emerald mines, timber fields, and marble quarries. Taxation, such as a 100 percent tax on cigarettes, provides some funds as well, and ransoms from kidnappings provide more. Though some nations have declared that they will not pay demanded ransoms to keep from further funding the Taliban, ransom money still brings in revenue. "Protection" fees, which are essentially an extortion plot wherein the Taliban offers protection to businesses and communities in exchange for cash, are also a source of funds.

Some of the funding for the Taliban comes from the very people who are fighting them. The United States, one of the forces that deploys troops to fight the Taliban, sends funds to Pakistan as financial and military aid. The US has sent more than twenty billion dollars (possibly closer to forty billion dollars if including indirect funding sources) since 2001 because Pakistan is an important ally. Pakistan, in turn, provides funding to the Afghan Taliban. Pakistan's Inter-Service Intelligence (ISI) has helped with Taliban smuggling. Between the ISI and other independent contractors, significant portions of US aid have been turned over to the Taliban. Those funds then give the Taliban power and enable them significant influence over Afghanistan to this day. The Taliban is rich, and because it is rich, it is powerful.

The Resistance

During its rise, the Taliban did not go unopposed. Resistance within Afghanistan came in the form of the Northern Alliance, consisting of many of the warlords fighting the Taliban for power. Also known as the United Islamic Front for Salvation of Afghanistan (UIFSA), the Northern Alliance was a congregation of different militias formed by warlords whose goal was to dissolve the Taliban so that they could take over the country. The Northern alliance primarily consisted of three ethnic groups: Tajiks, Uzbeks, and Hazaras.

In 2001, the leader of the Northern Alliance, Ahmad Shah Masoud, was killed by two assumed Taliban or al-Qaeda members, but the group managed to survive Masoud's death. Both sides of the fight had allies, and Western influences backed the Northern Alliance. Sponsors included Iran, Russia, India, Tajikistan, the United States, and the United Kingdom. United States troops, the Afghan military, and the Northern Alliance all collaborated and managed to oust the Taliban from Kabul and regain control over much of Afghanistan in 2001.

The Revolutionary Association of Women of Afghanistan, or RAWA, is also one of the strongest opponents of the Taliban. RAWA is a group of socially and politically active women fighting for human rights and social justice. The Taliban's consistent infringement on women's rights and human rights is strongly protested by the women in RAWA. By providing aid to the women and children who were victims of the Taliban, RAWA was integral to the fight against the Taliban and the revitalization of Afghanistan after their removal.

External forces also took a hands-on role in fighting the Taliban. The United States and other Western nations joined the battle against terror in the 1990s and 2000s. Motivated by the belief that the Taliban was protecting the known al-Qaeda terrorist Osama bin Laden, who had helped coordinate the 9/11 terror attacks on the Pentagon and the World Trade Center, the United States began the war on terror. It was support from the United States and other Western allies that ultimately unseated the Taliban in 2001.

Different Perspectives on a Reign of Terror

Afghanistan's relationship with the Taliban is complex. The country was in the midst of a long and arduous civil war when the Taliban began their rise to power. Though the sharia law instilled by the Taliban was one of the most severe and limiting forms to take place in the Muslim world, violence had become a way of life during the years of Soviet occupation and civil war. The Taliban, with its highly structured ways and strict laws, was in many ways welcomed. The peace the Taliban brought was refreshing after such great turbulence. One teen named Nasimi, in an interview with the nonprofit group PRI, described this period by saying, "We wanted an end to the warlords, and we wanted national unity. The Taliban gave us that." Nasimi went so far as to say, "It was a golden time. There was nothing to distract you—no cinema, no snooker parlors, not too many people in the streets. You could catch your breath." After years of civil war, any form of peace would have seemed a relief, and the strict sharia law ensured that crime rates dropped dramatically.

For some, however, the suffering under the Taliban was intense and was not welcomed. Women faced the most obvious and, in some cases, debilitating changes under

Taliban rule. One girl, Shukria, remembers the years of Taliban control with a much different perspective than Nasimi. She said in an interview with PRI, "I still remember those seven years, when I was locked up at home. I fell so far behind in terms of development. I was in a prison—I could not even go to the market without a *mahram*." To not be able to leave her home without a male family member as an escort was a very different experience from Nasimi's experience of quiet streets and peace. Furthermore, violence was always a threat under the Taliban because sharia law is very in tune with the idea of "an eye for an eye." Shukria continued describing her experience with, "One day I was shopping, and I [had] on a long chador instead of a [burka]. We came upon a group of Taliban. One of them took off his shoe and hit me with it a couple of times, asking 'why are you not wearing a [burka]?' Then they turned on my *mahram* and kicked him." For simply going out dressed differently than the Taliban demanded, Shukria and her *mahram* were attacked. As someone who was shut in because of Taliban orders, Shukria said that rather than living through Taliban rule again, she would kill herself if they ever came back.

These two experiences are just short examples of the complex relationships that different people had with Taliban control. For some, the Taliban was a return to quieter, more peaceful times and the devout, religious life they preferred. For other people, especially many women and girls, it was a time of imprisonment and limitation. To fully understand the complex social environment that allowed the Taliban to come to power, it's important to go back and examine the horrors of Soviet occupation and civil war. It is only then that the rise of the Taliban in Afghanistan truly makes sense.

Taken in 1980, Rikio Imajo's *Crowded Sidewalk in Kabul* shows life in Kabul, Afghanistan, under the Soviet-supported government right before American journalists were ordered out of the country for "biased reporting."

CHAPTER TWO

A CLOSER LOOK AT THE RISE OF THE TALIBAN

Terror organizations do not simply appear. Typically, the rise of terror organizations is not an unexpected or even a quick process. The circumstances that lead to the development of terror groups begin years in advance, and terror organizations often arise out of power vacuums. When a government loses control, and there is no suitable replacement, the country becomes vulnerable. That lack of leadership creates an opportunity for a coup, and sometimes those coups are violent. This is what happened in Afghanistan. A series of weak governments left the nation vulnerable to dangerous external and internal influences. It all began with a monarch—and ended with the horrors of terrorism.

WEALTH AND OIL

Afghanistan has some of the richest stores of unused natural resources of anywhere in the world. It is estimated that these resources, which include mineral deposits of iron ore, gold, natural fuel, and copper, amount to about three trillion US dollars. Natural fuel stores include both oil and gas. Since 2013, Afghanistan has started tapping these riches in the hopes of building up its economy. However, there are some challenges standing in the way. Warlords and the Taliban alike make it difficult for the country to leverage its assets. Ensuring the security of resources from insurgents is just one facet of the challenge.

Because Afghanistan is one of the poorest nations in the world, such stores offer important opportunities for growth and development. Growth would benefit both the government and its people. However, as it stands, opium monopolizes a lot of Afghanistan's resources and trade. The Taliban is not willing to risk losing the wealth that comes from the drug trade. Unfortunately for the government, dependence on drug trafficking often scares off businesses looking to harvest Afghanistan's natural resources, minerals, and fuel sources. If Afghanistan can find a way to safely access its natural resources, then great wealth—and greater stability—could follow.

A History of War

Afghanistan has a long history of domination and occupation by other nations. During the eighteenth-century colonial era, the country was annexed by Britain. A series of wars, known as the British-Afghan Wars, ensued as the Afghani people fought for independence. It took until the end of World War II for that dream of independence to be realized. A monarchy was put in place, and Amir Amanullah Khan became king. Khan, however, abdicated his throne when the people rose up after he tried to limit the power of the country's national council.

After Khan's abdication, Zahir Shah assumed the throne in 1933. Shah was a successful king, but in 1953, Soviet influence took hold in Afghanistan. This was the Cold War era, and communism was spreading quickly. Shah's cousin, General Mohammad Daud Khan, was a Soviet supporter and became prime minister. His connections to the Soviet Union began supplying military support, and progressive changes for women's rights began. Women were allowed greater social and economic opportunities than ever before. They were able to work and attend universities. Western fashion became more common, and Afghanistan under Shah was different from ever before. Then, in the mid-1950s, the Soviet Union officially allied with Afghanistan. By 1965, the Afghan Communist Party formed. Afghanistan was changing rapidly yet again, and the next twenty years would bring even more extreme differences.

In 1973, General Khan successfully overthrew his cousin in a military coup. General Khan then transformed Afghanistan into the Republic of Afghanistan while declaring himself president. Like his cousin's, his leadership was progressive and pushed for women's rights as well as modernization, but President Khan was not in power for long. In 1978, the Afghan Communist Party staged a coup and overthrew the government yet again. President Khan was killed, and the leaders of the party, Nur Mohammad Taraki and Babrak Karmal, were named president and deputy prime minister. Ties with the Soviet Union remained friendly through it all.

Next, division in the government and nation exploded. Communist rivals split the party, and fighting broke out between them. On one side was President Taraki and on the other was rival Hafizullah Amin. Meanwhile, in the more rural areas, a guerrilla group, the mujahideen, began to rise as well, seeking to protest the progressive changes put in place under President Khan. They also wanted to replace the government for having Soviet ties.

The nation destabilized quickly. In September of 1979, President Taraki was killed by Amin's supporters, and a new power vortex arose. The communist government was failing without the president and in the face of all the infighting. The USSR, looking to preserve its communist presence in the Middle East, was quick to get involved and invaded in December of that year. Babrak Karmal was named prime minister in an attempt to fill the void left by Taraki. The country's citizens were furious. The Soviet presence and Taraki's control were violently protested. At the start of the next year, the mujahideen mobilized against the government and Soviets. They were backed by the USSR's Cold War enemy, the United States, by way of Pakistan. Support from Pakistan and the United States helped fuel the resistance. It was 1978, and the civil war had officially begun.

Within just two years, the mujahideen controlled the rural areas while the Soviets maintained the cities. In order to avoid the war, people were fleeing the country to the nearby nations of Pakistan and Iran. It is estimated that 4.3 million people fled the country during this period. It was a violent time, with bombings of civilian areas by the Soviets. They hoped that by attacking civilians they would be able to eliminate public support for the rebels. Their efforts failed. It only angered people further that somewhere between 800,000 and 1.5 million people died, both soldiers and civilians alike, during the occupation. Back in the USSR, there was also trouble. By the end of the 1980s, the USSR was floundering. The government was losing control of their country as well as Afghanistan. Military arms support for the mujahideen came from nations including the United States, Great Britain, and China, and the Soviets' hold continued to weaken. Pakistan, as an ally, accepted refugees.

On the opposition side, the mujahideen was only growing stronger. To further exacerbate the problem for the Soviets, al-Qaeda briefly joined the fight against them, and Soviet power continued to slip. By 1989, the USSR withdrew from Afghanistan and declared it an independent state in hopes of focusing its energies on its own waning power at home. The mujahideen had gotten what they wanted. The communist government that was left in place in Afghanistan, however, did not. It was not strong and had little chance of standing against the mujahideen. In 1992, without Soviet support, the government fell to the mujahideen. Once again, a new power vortex arose. Warlords from different sections of Afghanistan began fighting for power and control. Violence and war raged around the country as different factions fought to control the whole nation. The warlords committed atrocities. Afghanistan was slowly being ripped apart. More than anything, people were dying in large numbers every day. Afghanistan was ravaged by militias and yet another war, this time a civil war. By this point, the nation had been at war for more than twenty years.

Taliban Rising

The people of Afghanistan had now experienced years of conflict and war. Many Afghani people were growing up in refugee camps in Pakistan rather than their own country. The constant fighting meant everyone was in danger, and death tolls were high. That kind of exhaustion meant any peace would have been welcomed, and a form of peace did come this time: the Taliban.

The insurgency of the Taliban had begun gathering support during Soviet occupation, but the infighting and power plays of the warlords allowed it to truly grow. The country was left with a desperate desire for stability that made the Taliban ideology and strict enforcement of laws all too appealing. War had not raged so long that people did not remember a different way of life, and the desire for the elusive quiet of peace was intensified with every bomb that dropped. The Taliban, with its devout and severe Islamic ideology, seemed to offer an opportunity to end the seemingly constant stream of endless wars.

The Taliban consists mostly of Pashtun people, and the opposition is mostly non-Pashtun. The Pashtun ethnic group is the majority group in Afghanistan and originates from the Afghan and Pakistani border in both countries. The Pashtuns are primarily from the northeast portion of the

This photo, titled *Civil War in Afghanistan,* was taken in 1989. It shows the ravaged streets of Jelalabad.

nation, though some tribes have moved into Pakistan. It is important to note that though the Taliban tends to consist of mostly Pashtun people, not all Pashtun people are with or support the Taliban. In fact, in 2012, a Taliban spokesman named Umar Muhammad insisted that the Taliban was a Muslim movement, not a Pashtun one. That said, there have been ethnic cleansing and religious intolerance and persecution on both sides of these battles.

In 1994, the Taliban, with its religious scholars and military strength, swept in with its vicious justice. The Taliban succeeded where the warlords had failed; they took over the nation. Essentially, the Taliban disbanded the individual militias one by one, fighting off the warlords and gradually restoring order to the country, one section at a time. They replaced the judicial system with the most stringent form of sharia law ever seen in any Islamic nation. According to foreign policy expert Ahmed Rashid, within the first twenty-four hours of taking the capital, Kabul, the strident sharia law that now embodies the code of the Taliban was in place.

The tradeoff for peace was a staunchly religious society that limited many of the freedoms and rights of the people. The Taliban ruled through might and used violence to control the populace, but the streets were safer than they had been since the Soviets' arrival.

Afghanistan was once again a wholly different land. The rapes and abductions that took place during the wars ceased, but punishments for anything seen as immoral were terrible. Under the Taliban, a man could be beaten or jailed if his beard was too short. Under the Taliban, women were forbidden from most education, and education for boys was solely religious. Furthermore, religious police scoured the city to ensure that people did not miss the calls to prayer. If they did, they faced terrible consequences.

In many ways, violence was the ultimate tool of the Taliban. Sharia law allowed for painful and brutal consequences, but it was also a controlled violence. The Taliban were the only ones who could mete out punishments, as opposed to the threat of violence from multiple factions during the civil war.

During the civil war, theft was a large problem. Under the Taliban's rule, thieves could lose a hand for stealing—

meaning that few people stole. The streets were far safer than before because the greatest threat was the strict and brutal consequences for violating the laws.

Allies Over the Border

During the Afghan Soviet occupation and civil war, Pakistani sympathizers became great allies. Afghani militants and refugees alike found safe havens over the border. That support grew as the years continued and transformed those allies into Taliban sympathizers once the Taliban rose in Afghanistan. From those factions rose the Pakistani Taliban. Though smaller and less centrally organized than their Afghan counterparts, the Taliban in Pakistan continue to be allied and supporters of the Afghan Taliban. Their ideology is much the same: consistent with sharia law and brutal justice. Though they have never been as dominant in Pakistan as the Afghan Taliban came to be in Afghanistan, the Pakistani Taliban are just as violent and dangerous as the Afghan Taliban.

Pakistan's Taliban

It is important to note Pakistan's relationship with Afghanistan during the early years and since the turn of the millennium. They have been interesting allies, as have their terrorist organizations. The Pakistani Taliban, once known as the Tehrik-i-Taliban Pakistan (TTP), has been sanctioned by the UN just as the Afghan Taliban has.

The Pakistani Taliban often provides support to the Taliban in Afghanistan. During the Soviet conflict, they would send men to help fight and would provide military weapons and aid. Though the two groups use very similar methods and share ideology, the goal of the Pakistani Taliban is far different from that of the Afghan Taliban. The main goal of the Pakistani Taliban is to overthrow the Pakistani government and replace it with a fundamental, Islamic one. Their interests do not really lie in Afghanistan. As a group, they are violent and oppressive.

In 2007, Pakistani Taliban leader Baitullah Mehsud coordinated the unification of the independent factions into a coalition of militias. Mehsud led the groups until his death by air strike in 2009. These groups continue to collaborate today.

Though their central goal is to overthrow the Pakistani government, the Pakistani Taliban will also attack countries allied with Pakistan. They have also killed civilians to make political points and under the guise of religious aims. They received worldwide attention for their attacks on young girls going to school in 2012, but that is not the end of their violence. They have also bombed mosques—places of peace and prayer. They will do just about anything to keep out foreign entities and to reach their goals.

The Pakistani Taliban is smaller than other terror organizations in the region. Their views do not fully align with those of the Afghan Taliban or al-Qaeda. Instead, their goals bridge between the other two terror organizations' perspectives. The Pakistani Taliban want to overthrow their government like the Taliban in Afghanistan do, but they also want to bring down the Western world and the United States, much like al-Qaeda. They operate close to the Afghanistan and Pakistan border in the Federally Administered Tribal Areas (FATA), and they are expanding outward from there. Their smaller size makes the goal of combating the West more challenging. This does not stop them from formulating and executing terror attacks in an attempt to do so both within the country and globally. In May of 2010, a Pakistani American, Faisal Shahzad, tried to detonate a car bomb in New York City's Times Square after being trained by the Pakistani Taliban on how to do so. The attack failed.

Under the Taliban

Sharia law has been implemented in other parts of the Muslim world, but never quite like the Taliban's extreme edicts in Afghanistan. Women were banned from work, even though they were one-fourth of the civil service sector. Ahmed Rashid notes that women had filled almost all of the positions in elementary education and occupied a large number of positions in the health field—and yet were completely barred from work as soon as the Taliban took control of Kabul in Afghanistan. Around seventy thousand female students were forbidden from getting an education,

In 1996, this woman had to wear a full burka in public due to the extreme Islamic law instated under the Taliban.

and schools for girls and women closed as soon as the Taliban took charge of the country. It did not even matter that, due to the war, there were thousands of families without a male head of the house, and the women were the primary providers. Women could no longer work, and for those families, there was no one to provide.

Anyone found consuming liquor was whipped, and adultery meant guilty parties were stoned to death. Murderers could and would be killed in turn by the families of their victims. There was little room for mercy.

SHAZIA RAMZAN

In October of 2012, three teenage girls boarded a bus on their way to school. They were talking about their test scores and had their books in hand when militants from the Pakistani Taliban opened fire on them. They were attacked simply for wanting the right to an education and for being friends with education activist Malala Yousafzai. One girl, Shazia Ramzan, was only fourteen when the Taliban shot her in the hand and shoulder for being near Malala. After this, Shazia had trouble sleeping for fear someone would come again and shoot her.

Under the Taliban, there was little freedom for young girls, and this is just one example of the Pakistani Taliban's atrocities. Girls could not swim, nor could they shop without a chaperone. Shazia described her hometown in the Swat District of Pakistan thusly, "Back home, you have to go anywhere with your father, mother or brother, because you are a girl." Even two years later, in 2014, Shazia had trouble understanding what had happened to her. She said in an interview, "Why were we hit by bullets, why? Because we were just girls? Why? Because we want just an education?" Unfortunately, under the Taliban, a desire for education was enough to justify such a response.

The Pakistani Taliban had similar rules but were most notorious for their banning of girls' educations. Though the Taliban in Afghanistan would also ban girls' education, there was a strong and passionate response to the banning in Pakistan. Educating a girl in Pakistan could potentially be a death sentence, but girls fought back. In fact, in both countries, women were some of the most active participants in the Taliban resistance.

Taking on the Taliban

The government and other factions continued to fight the Taliban. The Afghan military struggled to take on the well-funded Taliban, and the Northern Alliance formed by the warlords had even greater struggles. Unity did not come naturally to people who had so recently fought one another.

The support of other nations did help the resistance but not enough to reclaim the country. The Taliban simply kept battling back, and it had allies of its own. Saudi Arabia and Pakistan backed the Taliban. Alternatively, Iran, four nations in Central Asia, and Russia sent reinforcements to the resistance and threatened to intensify their support if the Taliban continued to move northward in Afghanistan. They were forced to follow through when the Taliban continued to expand, paying little mind to demands that the group stay in the south. Russia and Iran sent the resistance more military supplies in hopes that they would be able to stop the Taliban from gaining further control. It did not work.

Eventually, the anti-Taliban factions unified in a formalized political alliance. (The United Islamic and National Front for the Salvation of Afghanistan was formed on June 13, 1997. They went so far as to create a capital in Mazar and declare Burhanuddin Rabbani president.) Ahmad Shah Masoud, who had led the anti-Taliban alliance military, was also placed in a position of power. The alliance was prepared to formally resist and fight the Taliban. They would do so for years.

The rest of the world was also vocal about the Taliban's actions, especially when they began receiving increased support from nearby nations, specifically Saudi Arabia. In 1996, the United States sent the assistant secretary of state for South Asia, Robin Raphel, to explore the state of Afghanistan as well as secure US economic interests in the oil industry. The United States urged the Afghani people and the Taliban to find peace, but these statements had no effect. When that strategy failed, Raphel and the United States urged the United Nations to place an arms embargo on Afghanistan in the hope of forcing peace. The embargo did not move forward, but eventually the UN was forced to speak up.

Taliban militants drive a tank just outside of Kabul in February 1995, a year before the Taliban took control of the nation's capital.

When the Taliban took Kabul on September 26, 1996, the United Nations had no choice but to intervene. That September day, the Taliban hanged the former Afghani president, Najibullah. He had been granted diplomatic immunity and was living in a UN compound in Kabul. Najibullah and his brother were killed as means of scaring the city. The world at large, but specifically the Muslim world, condemned these killings. The UN also condemned the Taliban for their actions and placed sanctions on them. Unfortunately, the Taliban responded by calling for more executions of high-ranking opposition officials.

Feminist groups also became more vocal about the Taliban in 1997 after efforts to provide humanitarian aid to Afghan women and children became nearly impossible. The European commissioner for humanitarian affairs, Emma Bonino, and nineteen Western journalists were arrested for photographing women in a hospital. Photography of women had been banned under the Taliban, and the arrests garnered a lot of public attention for women's issues.

Feminist organizations in the United States soon started lobbying in Washington. Up to this point, President Bill Clinton's administration had been lenient and avoided taking a stand against the Taliban. Lobbyists began protesting in Washington in support of Afghani women. Secretary of State Madeleine Albright went so far as to publicly denounce the Taliban. The Taliban grew increasingly opposed to Western ideas because of Western intervention.

Shortly thereafter, the United Nations addressed the Taliban once again. According to Ahmed Rashid in his book *Taliban*, on December 8, 1998, the UN Security Council Resolution on Afghanistan "threatened unspecified sanctions against the Taliban for harboring international terrorists, violating human rights, promoting drugs trafficking and refusing to accept a cease-fire."

Three years later, September 11, 2001, would force the United States to take action against the group. The terror attacks on September 11 were staged by al-Qaeda. Osama bin Laden, the leader of al-Qaeda, was residing in Afghanistan at the time. After the attacks, the United States approached the Taliban, demanding Osama bin Laden be turned over to be tried for the crimes. The Taliban refused, saying they did not trust that bin Laden would receive a fair trial. They

Emma Bonino was arrested in 1997 for photographing women under Taliban rule.

demanded that bin Laden be sent to an unbiased Islamic country for trial. The American government refused. Tensions mounted. Ultimately, Mullah Omar did not turn over Osama bin Laden. The United States subsequently declared war with Afghanistan in October of that year as a means to seek out bin Laden—as well as to punish the Taliban for protecting him.

The very first air strike after the declaration of war hit Mullah Omar's home. Omar survived, but his ten-year-old son did not. The death of his son would send Omar into hiding for years until his own death. War began in Afghanistan once again, but no one could have imagined how long it would rage.

Oleg Nikishin's 2002 photo shows a group of men and a young boy, part of the Afghan National Alliance, standing armed in front of the village of Jabul os Sarache.

CHAPTER THREE

YOUNG RECRUITS

In 2009, journalist Anand Gopal met with one of the leaders of a Taliban unit known as Mullah Cable in Gayawa, Afghanistan. Mullah Cable was feared and notorious. He carried a whip constructed out of a cable and used it liberally to maintain order. He wore glasses, had gold teeth, and was missing an eye from his years of fighting. He led a militant group that caused a great deal of damage. His men assassinated members of the Afghan government for having United States support, he helped coordinate and execute kidnappings of people such as policemen, and he and his men also deployed suicide bombers in the name of jihad. Like most Taliban members, he wanted foreigners out of Afghanistan and hoped for the Taliban regime to gain control of the country.

Interestingly, Mullah Cable had no religious education and was not fully literate. Prior to waging jihad, he had little knowledge of Americans or the United States. He was a young child when the Soviet forces arrived, and he enlisted in the local militia when they left in 1992. He joined the Taliban for a period but left the group briefly after the Americans invaded Afghanistan. For a short while, he even supported the Afghani government that the United States had helped put in place. Later, he rejoined the Taliban. Though he was not what anyone would necessarily expect of a Taliban leader, he worked his way up the ranks nonetheless.

How Mullah Cable ended up a notorious Taliban leader makes sense in context. He had grown up in the era of the warlords and was sick of the violence and infighting. The Taliban offered a welcome haven against the warlords, as well as purpose and unity. Mullah Cable said, "You have to understand, we felt like we were the most powerful people in the world. Everyone was talking about the Taliban. The whole world knew about the Taliban. We brought good to this country. We brought security. Before we came, even a trip to buy groceries was a gamble. People stole, people raped, and no one could say anything."

By 2001, Mullah Cable was leading a large group on the front lines and was responsible for disarming the public in new territories. That was what the whip was used for. It was obvious that he was devout, and it is apparent that the lure of the Taliban is complex. There was a sense of glory, there was power, and most of all, there was peace. Any of those things could be a draw for people who had seen their country ravaged by war. One of the most effective weapons of the Taliban was harder to understand: suicide bombers. On September 9, 2001, while Mullah Cable was leading at the front lines, the Taliban used the first suicide bomber from Afghanistan. With that successfully detonated bomb, the Taliban found a possible method to maintain their power.

Suicide bombers became a valuable and powerful weapon, but the use of suicide bombers was a contradiction. Islam is not a religion that sanctions suicide. It is explicitly prohibited in the Quran. Even Mullah Omar was against suicide bombings, preferring roadside bombs. That said, the success of such methods was undeniable and ensured that they became a regular practice of the Taliban. From then on, the Taliban began seeking out people willing to sacrifice themselves in the name of jihad.

Jihad and the Child Suicide Bomber

Suicide bombers have been used with great regularity since 2005 and are a popular tool for Taliban insurgents in both Afghanistan and Pakistan. Their continued success is due in part to the use of children. Children are an important aspect of the Taliban's military plans. Children of all ages are used to recover dropped weapons, rescue wounded soldiers, and serve as spies and suicide bombers. Between 2004 and 2014, 250 children were arrested by Afghan forces for working with the Taliban.

Unfortunately, children are uniquely vulnerable to Taliban recruiting. They are young and impressionable. Furthermore, children are accessible. Many boys in Afghanistan attend schools called madrasas. Madrasas house young boys, provide them with food, and also provide them with a religious education. The Taliban has had success recruiting from madrasas. In other cases, children are also taken off the streets or chosen from poor areas and neighborhoods. Usually male children are chosen and recruited, but there have been some cases of girls also being recruited.

From there, the children are taken and trained by the Taliban. They are told lies, and they are brainwashed by propaganda until they are willing to take violent action.

Madrasas, such as the one depicted here in Kabul, Afghanistan, are Islamic schools for boys.

In order to garner their trust and convince them that they are doing the right thing, the Taliban tells children that suicide attacks will earn them a place in heaven. They make participation seem exciting and interesting. Kids are promised paradise in exchange for their actions, and their actions are justified with yet more lies. Taliban insurgents tell recruits that foreign forces are abusing Afghan women and that Americans burn the Islamic holy book, the Quran. Promises of securing places in paradise for their whole families are also offered in exchange for fighting the foreign invaders. To justify civilian deaths to the children, they are told that the civilians killed are Afghans who were not devoted enough or not "true Muslims" because they work with Americans and therefore they deserve to die. They are trained to hurt and kill, and sometimes they are clueless about what they are doing because they are lied to. Children are told that they will not feel pain when the bombs go off. They are convinced that they cannot be hurt, and are invincible, by Afghan militants who shoot them with fake bullets or bury them alive and then bring them back to safety. These actions are used to convince older children that they can and will rise from the dead once their mission is accomplished.

One ten-year-old boy named Naqibullah was taken from his madrasa and held by Taliban men for months in a different school. Then, in Naqibullah's words, "One day they took me in a car [to Kandahar], gave me a heavy vest to wear and pointed to [some] soldiers." Luckily for Naqibullah, he was arrested before he reached the designated location and exploded his vest, but the men who brought him escaped by driving off. They left him to be arrested by the authorities. In the case of Naqibullah and many others, parents and guardians are often not aware that their child has been recruited. A child will suddenly go missing for weeks or months at a time. Some are never seen again, while others are randomly returned. In some of these cases, parents will even turn their children over to authorities after long, unexplained absences for fear that they have been brainwashed by the Taliban and recruited.

Unfortunately for survivors of such radicalization, there is little understanding of how to help children once they have been recruited. There are not many resources to help such children, and some even admit to regretting not being able to finish the mission they were sent out to complete. As of 2014, there were thirty children held in detention facilities by Afghan authorities because they were affiliated with Taliban missions. In 2015, the Ministry of Justice had 214 boys detained in juvenile rehabilitation centers, and 166 more children were detained in a facility in Parwan for the same reason. Of those numbers, fifty-three children were under the age of eighteen. But there is little that can be done to help the children assimilate to normal Afghan life. Charu Lata Hogg, the director of Child Soldiers International (a human rights group specifically interested in child soldiers), noted that as of 2015, "There's nothing to support their rehabilitation, whether psychological, physical, emotional, or educational. There is absolutely no service in place at the moment." Families do seem to help with reintegration when they are present, but that is only if there is family to be found.

According to Dr. Mia Bloom, a professor at Georgia State University, rehabilitating such children "will require a level of coordination and creativity not seen in any de-radicalization program so far … requiring a multipronged approach that addresses the psychological trauma suffered by the children and … re-education so they can unlearn distortions of the Islamic faith." As of 2017, exact methods for such deradicalization had yet to be developed.

The Unique Vulnerability of Child Soldiers

In 2017, Afghan police discovered and arrested a human trafficking ring that had kidnapped twenty-five children for the Afghanistan Taliban to use as suicide bombers. The youngest child was four years old; the oldest child was merely fourteen. The children appeared to be drugged, and many of them were orphans from Ghazni. The ring was trying to take the children into Pakistan to the city of Quetta, where Afghan leaders would begin training the children.

In this case, the use of madrasas and the death of these children's parents made the children especially vulnerable to recruitment. Madrasas are free to students and provide shelter as well as an education, making them most valuable to poor families. Furthermore, the Taliban is wealthy and can offer financial help to poor families, who are therefore vulnerable to coercion. A family receives money or protection in exchange for a child. Dr. Bloom says the Taliban uses extortion to take children from families. The Taliban has the resources to demand incredible amounts of money from a

This photo, taken of two children in Afghanistan in 2017, shows the continued plight of children and families who lack economic opportunity.

family or instead demand one of their children, so families are forced to choose a child to surrender. In other situations, in exchange for a child's service, a family could receive financial compensation or prestige. Cash, guns, cellular phones, and protection are traded for children. The Taliban use the poor population's desperation against them. Bloom states that terrorist groups rely "on an environment in which there's hopelessness, and lack of feeling there's a future ahead of you, so what they're promising is an afterlife in which everything is perfect." Lured by sweets and food, children are taught they are helping the country and doing something for the betterment of everyone.

Children in Taliban families or those with Taliban ties are particularly vulnerable. Children with male family members involved in the Taliban are more likely to fight with the Taliban as they have been raised in an environment that fosters allegiance to the Taliban and their jihad.

Child Soldiers on All Sides

It's not just the Taliban that recruits child soldiers. In actuality, child soldiers are used on both sides of the fight because the Afghan government uses child recruits as well. The poverty in some areas makes the salary earned from working with the government appealing to children and families. Add in patriotism and prestige with such work, and joining the Afghan National Police (ANP) or the Afghan Local Police (ALP) is very enticing. A child working for the ALP can earn between $103 and $155 monthly. The ANP is even more lucrative, with the capacity to earn between $172 and $310.

The United Nations reported at least sixty-eight cases of children being used by either the Taliban or the Afghan government in 2014. The government had vowed not to recruit children in 2011, but children are still fighting. In February of 2016, the *Los Angeles Times* reported the death of a renowned child soldier.

This Pashtun child is a member of the mujahideen and represents just one of many children forced into battle.

OUTLAWING THE USE OF CHILD SOLDIERS

In 1989, the United Nations Convention on the Rights of the Child declared that any person under the age of eighteen was a child. In Afghanistan, there are also laws prohibiting the use of children in war: specifically, a boy without a beard cannot fight. It is even considered a war crime to enlist children under the age of fifteen. This edict has been in place since 2002 under the Rome Statute of the International Criminal Court and includes both formal military and participation in informal militias. Prior to 2002, the prohibition of child soldiers under the age of fifteen was forbidden by the 1949 Geneva Convention at the close of World War II. The Optional Protocol to the Convention on the Rights of the Child (OPAC) also stated in 2000 that no one under the age of eighteen could be recruited in armed groups and militias that are not state sanctioned.

Even with all that legal protection in place, child soldiers are still used in Afghanistan. According to Human Rights Watch, an international organization, there are reports that children enrolled in Taliban religious schools start learning military skills as early as six years old. By the time they are thirteen, these recruits can create and deploy an IED (improvised explosive device) as well as use a firearm.

When Wasil Ahmad was nine, his father was killed by Taliban militants. In response, he learned how to operate and fire an AK-47 rifle. He wanted to get revenge on the people who killed his father. By the time of his death at the age of twelve, he was well known for killing Taliban militants, even killing six people in a matter of two months. Though still a boy, he felt he had to fight like a grown man and died because of it. Ahmad was killed by two men while waiting at a fruit stand. A local police commander justified Ahmad's fighting by saying, "He had to take up arms. He was defending his home, his family."

It is difficult to tell just how widespread the use of child soldiers is because records are not often kept—or shared with international reporting groups. However, some documents show the recruitment of 556 boys and 4 girls from September of 2010 to December of 2014 by oppositional groups in Afghanistan. There were 320 documented youth deaths and 950 injuries to children during the first six months of 2015 alone.

Fighting for Glory

Another reason young people join the Taliban is the honor associated with joining. As with Mullah Cable, to many, the Taliban represents an opportunity for glory and excitement.

These factors can draw a vulnerable young person to the Taliban. Religious motivations also play significant roles.

In 2007, reporter Sean Langan filmed *Meeting the Taliban*. In the documentary, Langan interviewed a teenage boy who was both armed and prepared to fulfill a mission of suicide bombing. The young man had a bomb strapped to his chest that he was waiting to deploy on the orders of the Taliban. He was fifteen years old.

The fifteen-year-old said he was motivated by the desire to give his life for Islam. In the interview, Langan noted that Islam was a religion of peace and asked the boy to explain how such an act coincided with the peaceful edicts of the Islamic faith. The boy responded that his actions were necessary "because we have foreigners here, and we want to expel them."

When asked about his parents, the boy said they were proud of him and happy that he would be given orders by the Taliban. One of his brothers had already been "martyred," and his other siblings were all younger than him. As it turns out, the boy's father was a Taliban commander and assured Langan that his father (the boy's grandfather) had died in the name of Islam, and that he and the boy would do so as well. The commander stressed that such an act was a choice, one they were both willing to make for the sake of Islam. Of course, the version of Islam touted by the Taliban does not align with the dictates of the Quran. Only a tiny percentage of Muslims hold these radical views.

Calls to Join

The Taliban in Afghanistan, as well as the Pakistani Taliban, use a lot of propaganda to garner support from people of all ages, but especially from young people. Boys in Taliban-controlled madrasas are shown propaganda videos to begin brainwashing them. These videos are also used to show the power and strength of the organization to breed fear. Some videos are as simple as Taliban caravans traveling in broad daylight unhindered. Such a video shows that the insurgents have such a strong hold on certain areas that they do not even worry about Afghan troops, even though they are obviously a Taliban convoy. An example of one location where the Taliban operates openly is in Nimruz in southwest Afghanistan. Nimruz is a hub for drug trafficking and is controlled by the Taliban. There is little fear of opposing forces there.

Other propaganda methods rely on more blatant scare tactics. Videotaping the violent acts that the Taliban use to enforce their sharia law is a terrifying means of ensuring compliance. Videotapes of beatings, beheadings, and suicide bombers are spread through social media and other sites

RECRUITING FROM AFAR

The Taliban manipulates the minds of children and teens within Afghanistan and Pakistan through madrasas, but their methods for recruiting outside of the Middle East are much different. The internet is the main tool they use to reach out to young people in more distant lands. Using posts written in English on social media sites like Twitter and Facebook, the Taliban seeks to reach a larger, global audience with their extremist messages. In 2016, the Taliban even launched a short-lived app for Android devices that was designed to spread their messages more rapidly.

They use different languages as well. The website Voice of Jihad has recordings in Arabic, Urdu, English, and other Afghan languages. Abdul Sattar Mawnadi is an administrator for Taliban websites and said, "Wars today cannot be won without media. (Media) is directed to the heart rather than the body, while the weapon is directed to the body. If the heart is defeated, the battle is won and the body is defeated."

Essentially, the goal of using such tools is to target people through their emotions, which coincides with the methods the Taliban has always used to recruit new members. Knowing the value of propaganda, the insurgents now have a budget dedicated to media efforts. Troubled teens throughout the world could be vulnerable to such recruitment methods.

Brightly colored anti-American propaganda posters are displayed in the office of the Pakistani Taliban party.

on the internet. Depictions of Taliban convoys traveling in broad daylight and unthinkable acts of violence are tools to manipulate the public into viewing the Taliban as a strong and growing organization.

The Taliban's propaganda strategy evolves over time. After the Taliban regime fell in 2001, propaganda efforts focused on demonizing the United States and Western ways of life. However, in 2015, when US President Barack Obama began talking about demilitarizing Afghanistan and withdrawing troops, the propaganda changed. Since then, a great deal of propaganda is designed to smear the current government by painting government officials as unethical. One such example was criticizing local police for the way they handled criminal offenses. The Taliban worked to exaggerate criminal offenses to make the police appear as if they were failing to adequately handle crime.

Understanding Teen Recruitment

Growing up in Afghanistan is increasingly challenging for young people. The resurgence of the Taliban and other dangerous terrorist groups poses growing threats. Children and teens are noticeable victims of the clashes between these groups and government forces. In 2009, UNICEF's regional director for South Asia, Daniel Toole, declared that "Afghanistan today is without a doubt the most dangerous place to be born." Infant death rates may have dropped somewhat with increased numbers of trained midwives after the Taliban's fall, but malnutrition rates were at 40.9 percent. There are also low rates of vaccination due to humanitarian groups' increasingly poor access to the nation.

In recent years, the Taliban has become more active, especially after United States forces began withdrawing from the region. Schools are a main target of insurgents, and madrasas are hunting grounds for children that can be brainwashed into carrying out suicide bombings. Propaganda tactics are only becoming more effective, and the use of children and teens in conflict and suicide bombings is becoming more common rather than less.

Taliban militants attacked this school in Peshawar, Pakistan, in December 2014, killing 132 students and injuring more than 100 people.

CHAPTER FOUR

THE CASUALTIES OF THE TALIBAN: LIVING WITH TERROR

In 2014, Pakistani Taliban militants attacked a school in Peshawar, Pakistan. A car blew up behind the school, alerting the school's security that something was wrong. Yet the car bomb was merely a diversion so insurgents could storm the school. The militants opened fire on classrooms with children in them. One boy, Mohammad Bilal, had been taking a math test when tthe shots erupted. He dove into the bushes to protect himself.

Meanwhile, men marched through the hallways declaring "God is great!" while others burst through the back door of the school's auditorium and started shooting. Children were found in the gym and were shot. Taliban members found children hiding beneath the benches in the school,

TERROR IN THE UNITED STATES

On September 11, 2001, the United States was shaken by the worst terrorist attack on American soil to date. Al-Qaeda members hijacked planes and flew them into the World Trade Center in New York City and the Pentagon in Washington, DC. The attacks killed nearly three thousand people and set the stage for one of the longest conflicts in United States history—what President George W. Bush would refer to as the war on terror. Conflict with Afghanistan over the surrender of September 11 mastermind Osama bin Laden would lead to the American invasion of Afghanistan within a month of the terror attack.

The media ran nonstop coverage of September 11, and as details unfolded, many began to fear Islam—and not just the extremist sects of the religion. In turn, Muslim Americans became vulnerable to discrimination and hate crimes.

The events of September 11 clearly demonstrate the complexity of terrorism. Though it was al-Qaeda, not the Taliban, that carried out the attacks, the Taliban played a key role in what followed. The decision to harbor Osama bin Laden brought US forces to Afghanistan, which in turn fostered an environment that radicalized new members of the Afghan population. Despite the distance between the United States and the Middle East, events in each region create shockwaves that are felt around the world—and that affect the day-to-day lives of people in both.

and fourteen-year-old Ahmed Faraz heard the order given to execute the hiding children. Faraz heard a Taliban militant say, "A lot of children are under the benches. Kill them."

In all, 132 children were killed by the Pakistani Taliban that day. The students who died were all between the ages of twelve and sixteen. Ten staff members and three soldiers were also killed, and more than one hundred people were injured. The attack was over in a matter of fifteen minutes.

The Taliban's only goal was to kill as many people as possible in the attack. This is just one example of the atrocities carried out by the Pakistani Taliban, and it was far from the first attack by the militants that targeted children or schools. The most famous attack had taken place two years prior on a makeshift bus where three teenage girls were shot simply for wanting to go to school.

Malala Yousafzai

On July 12, 1997, in the Swat Valley, Pakistan, Malala Yousafzai was born into a progressive home. Her mother and father valued education and encouraged their daughter to do the same. Her father, Ziauddin Yousafzai, was a teacher and taught Malala to love learning. In 2007, the Pakistani Taliban invaded and gained control of the Swat Valley. Within the year, the valley was a very different place. Media were banned, and strict Islamic law was implemented. Harsh punishments were meted out for any infraction or disobedience. It was completely different from the world Malala had been raised in. But it wasn't until December of the following year that Malala's world changed in a way she could not tolerate. That's when the Taliban closed her school.

In response, Malala published blog posts, expressing her unhappiness and anger over the closing of girls' schools in Pakistan. Then, violence intensified further in the area and Malala's family—as well as many others—were forced to flee for safety. It was at this time that Malala's blog drew the attention of the *New York Times*. Though she used a pen name to write the blog, when she was invited to be featured in a documentary about living in the Swat Valley and fighting for girls' rights to education in the face of the Taliban, she chose to do so. Participation in the documentary drew Taliban attention, but Taliban presence died down in the Swat Valley by November of 2011. The Yousafzai family returned home to reopen Malala's school. Malala also began a very public campaign fighting for girls' rights to education, speaking out against the Taliban's policy that girls should not be educated.

Her growing popularity soon made Malala a target of the Taliban. On October 9, 2012, they sought their revenge. Gunman boarded the bus that Malala and two of her friends took to get to school. They asked, "Who is Malala?" and opened fire on the girls. Malala was shot in her head, neck, and shoulder. Her two friends were also shot simply for being with her. Against the odds, Malala survived the attack after treatment in the United Kingdom. Though her recovery was long, painful, and challenging, Malala fought to survive and return to school. Rather than give up her mission to support girls' rights to education in the face of terror, she became a voice for girls everywhere who did not have access to education. For her efforts, in December of 2014, Malala was named the youngest recipient of the Nobel Peace Prize at only seventeen years old. Since then, Malala continues on her mission to fight for girls' rights to education. She has become a symbol of strength in the face of injustice.

Shut In

Malala Yousafzai was not the only young woman to write about the Taliban's reign. Known only by her pen name, Latifa was a young Afghani woman who was sixteen years old when the Taliban took the capital city of Kabul in 1996. She and her family survived bombings and violence, but the Taliban brought a different life for her and her mother. Kabul under the Taliban was a stark contrast to what she was used to, coming from an educated, middle-class family. She and all other girls were forced to wear full veils, covering every inch of themselves in a burka or chador, in order to leave the house.

She needed a male escort anywhere she went. Then, the Taliban closed all girls' schools. Suddenly, her mother and all women were banned from working.

Gone were the days of makeup and brightly colored clothes. Speaking with a young man was outlawed, and breaking that law meant she would have to be married. As soon as she turned fourteen, she became of marriageable age by Taliban

Latifa escaped Taliban rule in 2002 and went on to publish a memoir of her experiences.

standards. If a member of the Taliban had taken interest in her like one did in her cousin, she would have been forced to marry him.

Perhaps the biggest danger of all for women was that very few women were able to keep working in the medical field. Because the Taliban declared that male doctors could not treat female patients, women's access to health care plummeted. Latifa's mother attempted to treat women secretly in a hidden medical practice. When Latifa's mother herself fell ill, there was nowhere to go for treatment. The family was forced to travel to Pakistan so that Latifa's mother could receive medical care.

Ultimately, Latifa and some of her family members chose to flee to Paris in an attempt to tell the outside world about the way women are treated under the Taliban. She and others like her believed that the only way to resist the Taliban was to publicly bear witness to the atrocities committed. Latifa felt that people needed to know that the only access to education and health care for women came from secret schools and often secret clinics. Since telling her story was the only way to resist, Latifa wrote a memoir called *My Forbidden Face*. She did so under a pen name for her own safety.

RAWA and the Women's Resistance

Latifa and Malala are two more recent examples of women working against Taliban control of Afghanistan and Pakistan. The legacy of this kind of activism stretches back to the 1970s. The Revolutionary Association of the Women of Afghanistan (RAWA) refer to themselves as "the oldest political/social organization of Afghan women struggling for peace, freedom, democracy and women's rights in fundamentalism blighted Afghanistan since 1977." RAWA has fought for a democratic and secular government since their founding and have continued fighting for freedom under every leader, occupation, and organization that has been in power since its founding. RAWA both protests injustice and documents atrocities.

During the Taliban occupation of Kabul, the Kabul stadium became a site of Taliban justice. Executions of murderers and adulterers and the amputations of limbs of thieves and other criminals happened there with shocking regularity. The stadium was open to the public, and many people witnessed the punishments of others. RAWA members chose to attend in order to bring attention to the cruelty of the Taliban.

Zarmina

On November 17, 1999, RAWA reported on the murder of an Afghan woman in the Kabul stadium. Though photography was forbidden under Taliban law, RAWA members took pictures and documented the event. The woman, known only as Zarmina, was a mother of seven who had been accused of beating her husband to death with a hammer while he slept. Zarmina was to be executed for her crime. The Taliban code of justice stated that murderers should be killed by the family members of the victim.

According to Islamic law, however, a person could be forgiven for their crimes by the family of the victim. Zarmina's husband's family had forgiven her, but it was too late. The Taliban refused to stop the execution. Instead,

Zarmina's children watched and cried out for her as she was killed.

Zarmina had been a victim of severe abuse at the hands of her husband. A police officer with a Taliban brother, Zarmina's husband had changed from the man she had married. He had been mild-mannered and good. Though the marriage was arranged, Zarmina loved her husband. Unfortunately, over time he became violent. He abused Zarmina and their older daughters every night. Eventually, Zarmina and one of her daughters plotted to kill him. They couldn't take any more of his relentless violence. Zarmina drugged her husband but could not go through with actually killing him. It was her teenage daughter who committed the crime. Zarmina professed guilt to protect her child.

Life Under the Taliban for Women

Anton Antonowicz, a writer for the *Mirror Online*, explained the unique plight of Afghan women by saying, "Women had no rights in the Taliban Afghanistan. They existed only to obey. They were drones to bear children, cook, and satisfy men." Furthermore, the consequences for infractions for women were inhumane. Women would lose their fingertips if caught wearing nail polish or could be stoned to death for adultery or prostitution. There were huge limitations placed upon what a woman could do. As a women's rights

An Afghani couple flees the frontlines and fighting in November of 1996.

organization, RAWA paid special attention to the restrictions placed upon women under the Taliban. Here are just a few examples provided by RAWA:

Ban on women laughing loudly. (No stranger should hear a woman's voice.)

Ban on women wearing high-heeled shoes, which could produce sound while walking. (A man must not hear a woman's footsteps.)

Compulsory painting of all windows, so women cannot be seen from outside their homes.

Ban on flared (wide) pant-legs, even under a burka.

Listening to music.

Celebrating the traditional new year (Nowroz) on March 21. The Taliban proclaimed the holiday un-Islamic.

Keeping pigeons and playing with birds, which were described as un-Islamic. The violators would be imprisoned and the birds shall be killed [sic].

Using the internet, by both ordinary Afghans and foreigners.

Anyone who carries objectionable literature will be executed.

Anyone who converts from Islam to any other religion will be executed.

Non-Muslim minorities must [wear a] distinct badge or stitch a yellow cloth onto their dress to be differentiated from the majority Muslim population. (Just like what [the Nazis did] with Jews.)

Bibi Aisha's Story

Islamic law, as interpreted by the Taliban, was violent. Islam is a peaceful religion, but extremism has taken something good and distorted it to justify control and extreme violence. The brutal consequences dealt out by the Taliban under

Listening to music.

Celebrating the traditional new year (Nowroz) on March 21. The Taliban proclaimed the holiday un-Islamic.

Keeping pigeons and playing with birds, which were described as un-Islamic. The violators would be imprisoned and the birds shall be killed [sic].

Using the internet, by both ordinary Afghans and foreigners.

Anyone who carries objectionable literature will be executed.

Anyone who converts from Islam to any other religion will be executed.

Non-Muslim minorities must [wear a] distinct badge or stitch a yellow cloth onto their dress to be differentiated from the majority Muslim population. (Just like what [the Nazis did] with Jews.)

Bibi Aisha's Story

Islamic law, as interpreted by the Taliban, was violent. Islam is a peaceful religion, but extremism has taken something good and distorted it to justify control and extreme violence. The brutal consequences dealt out by the Taliban under sharia law were often swift and painful. Such was the case for one eighteen-year-old girl.

Bibi Aisha was married to a member of the Taliban under the *baad* custom to pay the so-called blood debt for her family. A blood debt means that someone killed a family member of another; in this case Aisha's uncle killed a member of the Taliban member's family. Under the custom of *baad*, a girl could be offered in marriage as reparation for the blood debt. Bibi Aisha's marriage resolved the blood debt but at a terrible cost.

Bibi Aisha was twelve when she was married, and her husband and his family were abusive. She was beaten and treated like a slave. After six years of abuse, she ran away, back to her family. Her husband, with the Taliban in tow, found her and forced her family to turn her over to them. She was jailed for five months until her husband took her into the mountains one night, and Taliban men tied her up. Acting under the orders of a Taliban commander, her husband cut off her ears and then her nose as a consequence for running away. As some cultures in Afghanistan believe that a man "loses his nose" if his wife betrays him, so too would that be her consequence. Bibi Aisha was left for dead in the mountain clearing where the heinous punishment had been carried out.

Bibi Aisha survived a vicious Taliban attack.

Bibi Aisha was helped by aid workers and the US military, and they managed to get her to a safe house for women funded by Women for Afghan Women (WAW). She was slated for reconstructive surgery but needed intensive psychological counseling through WAW before she was ready to undergo the procedure. Eventually, with help from doctors in the United States, Bibi Aisha was able to have her nose reconstructed. However, the emotional impact of such a vicious attack is more difficult to address.

Secret Schools

In 2002, just after the Taliban was unseated, it was estimated that Afghanistan's literacy rate among females was about 7 percent. That's the lowest literacy rate for females in the world. Yet the statistic is not surprising in a nation where the controlling power had outlawed the education of women. Under Taliban control, schools were closed and bombed, so the only way to receive any form of education as a female was in secret. Organizations like RAWA, and girls and women hungry to learn, played key roles in the resistance movement against the Taliban because of the issue of education.

It was a very serious infraction to be caught teaching women to read, but women and girls were determined. Secret schools, based in homes, opened in Pakistan and Afghanistan. RAWA specifically opened several schools that many women, especially older women, gravitated to with their husbands' blessings. Classes through RAWA were smaller in Afghanistan on account of the danger. There were only about four women to a class at a time, but classes in Pakistan could be larger, with closer to fifteen women in attendance. The desire to learn outweighed the fear of punishment for each girl and woman who studied in a secret school. Yet the dangers were very real. Even with precautions in place, these schools were often raided by police. There is also evidence that the Taliban poisoned at least one hundred girls simply for attending school.

Secret schools continued even after the Taliban was overthrown because the terror group still has a strong hold in some areas. Furthermore, many school buildings had been rendered unusable by the Taliban's bombings. In some areas, UNICEF hosts schools based out of canvas tents, but with the increasing influence of the Taliban, those schools could be targets. Taliban insurgents attack schools to this day, and the continued violence leads to school closures.

Seeking a formal education can be dangerous for children in Afghanistan. In Taliban-controlled regions, small, secret homeschools pop up to fill the void. Teachers put themselves in danger by going to these schools to try to educate children, both girls and boys alike. One example of a secret school can be found high up in the mountain village of Spina.

Spina had a strong Taliban influence even after the terror group was removed from power and from the capital. Women remained under the draconian rule of the Taliban there, but small and quiet acts of defiance against the strict edicts of the Taliban were commonplace. In this part of the country, literacy rates for both men and women are low. In 2012, two brothers began to feel that their female family members should be granted the opportunity of an education. Though the brothers were very conservative and devout themselves, even identifying with the some of the ideologies of the Taliban, they believed in education. The two men began quietly teaching classes in their home for their female relatives. The girls learned subjects like math, as well as how to read and write. Word spread among women and girls that the brothers were teaching. Soon, it became difficult to keep the classes small, even though everyone feared attracting Taliban attention. That did not stop the girls, though. Young girls between the ages of five and twelve had attended the classes in the beginning, but soon teenagers arrived. This was especially notable because under Taliban rule, girls past adolescence are not supposed to go out in public. The teens wanted to learn badly enough that they were willing to break several rules.

The school was simple. Girls sat on the ground on carpets while reading from the Quran. There was a chalkboard on the floor, and the girls had to share what few textbooks they had. There was no money for desks or additional supplies.

Even with veiled threats from the Taliban like notes left on the door, the brothers continued teaching. One parliamentarian, Shukria Barakzai, also ran a secret school under Taliban rule in the 1990s and described such ventures by saying, "It's risky for teachers and it's risky for the students, but these underground schools show the thirst people have for education under the Taliban."

The Long-Term Effects of the Taliban

There are of course long-term effects from the limitations placed on girls and women, as well as society as a whole. Young girls did not know if they would ever be able to be educated in the open without risking severe consequences. Widowed women who were forbidden to work had no way to provide for their families. Education rates and literacy rates—which were already low—continued to drop. Furthermore, many female doctors and health providers were not able to work under the Taliban, and no new doctors were being trained to fill the few positions still available in women's health care. Without proper health care for women, the number of female deaths has risen, and so have infant and child mortality rates.

Slowed Growth

Afghanistan has been changed by terror and the Taliban. It has been changed by war, international occupation, and the influence of both the Western world and the Taliban. Since the Taliban's total control over the nation ended in 2001, there remains an obvious cultural influence of their continued presence. Internationally, other nations experienced the growth of the digital age during the Taliban's reign. In Afghanistan, the Taliban had eradicated technology and media. No one had access to the internet until the Taliban fell from power. This means that Afghanistan is decades behind other nations technologically. Even ten years after the Taliban lost control of the country, only 1.25 million people had access to the internet. That is only 4 percent of a population of thirty million. As of 2016, only 9 percent of the population was using social media. In an era often defined by social media, that constitutes a significant difference from many other nations—both developed and developing. Only 2.7 million people in Afghanistan used a mobile phone and 4.1 million people—about 12 percent of the total population—were using the internet in 2016.

The Taliban's impact on the economy has also been long lasting. Ongoing conflict interferes with economic growth. The Taliban still controls the drug trade in Afghanistan, which remains a lucrative industry. Furthermore, there is a serious need for infrastructure and development due to the Taliban's violence. Agriculture is just one example of many. Though Afghanistan is situated in a breadbasket—an area known for having rich, fertile land—people are starving because farms need to be rebuilt. The nation needs to start rebuilding so that the democratic government can stand on its own, but the Taliban has limited the government's opportunities to do so. The Taliban is strategic about securing their interests. Instability in Afghanistan helps the terror group maintain their wealth. And in turn, this wealth funds plans to gain ground.

It is also important to reiterate that Afghanistan remains a very traditional and conservative country. Though the Taliban is no longer the country's official government, there are still many people who support and identify with strict Islamic law. The liberal values of the kings and presidents

DISPLACEMENT AND REFUGEES

The war in Afghanistan and Taliban occupation have led to a staggering number of displaced people. According to Amnesty International, as of 2016, there are 1.2 million internally displaced people (IDP)—people who have left their homes, but not their country, in the hope of finding safety. The refugee population is more than double that at 2.6 million people. Unlike IDP, refugees have fled their country. Ultimately, that means that more than 3.8 million people have been forced from their homes and must live their day-to-day lives in uncertain circumstances. The current Afghan government does not supply sufficient resources for internally displaced people. The internal camps lack proper resources like food, water, shelter, health care, education, and employment. One woman, Mastan, who lives in a camp in Herat, Afghanistan, said in reference to her shelter, "Even an animal would not live in this hut, but we have to. I would prefer to be in prison rather than this place, at least in prison I would not have to worry about food and shelter."

Refugees face similar problems. Limited resources are provided by host countries, but refugees seem to fare somewhat better than those who are displaced within Afghanistan. Many Afghan refugees have found themselves in camps in Pakistan and India, and they are forming communities there.

during the 1960s and 1970s are long past. The prevalent conservatism does not mean that there are not progressive people to be found in Afghanistan; it merely means that the Taliban has had a lasting impact on the country and culture as a whole. The Taliban is still an active and very influential part of Afghan life. Though the group does not have the majority control of the country anymore, they are present in many parts of it.

Things are different in Pakistan. There is not as much support for the Pakistani Taliban in the sense that it is not as large, though they are growing stronger. However, the Pakistani government did not reject the traditional ideology of the Taliban in Afghanistan; Pakistan was one of the few nations that supported the Taliban's power in Afghanistan and recognized the regime as legitimate leadership. Though the government continues to resist the Taliban efforts in their own country, Pakistan is definitely a conservative nation, and the fundamentalist ideology has found supporters in the FATA lands. Their numbers are growing, and despite their less-unified approach, they are gaining more ground. As of 2017, the UN has been watching the organization more closely and even discussed an embargo and freezing the assets of a splinter group of Pakistani Taliban.

The American military has been active in Afghanistan since 2001 and continues to combat Taliban insurgents. In December of 2017, Vice President Pence visited troops in Bagram Air Field in Afghanistan.

CHAPTER FIVE

SOLVING TERROR

October 2017 marked the sixteenth year of United States troops' presence in Afghanistan. This continued presence stems from the very real threat the Taliban still poses. Though the Taliban no longer holds 90 percent of the country like it did during its peak in the late 1990s, Taliban presence is steadily growing. The group continues to carry out attacks with shocking regularity. The Taliban was responsible for ninety-three terror attacks in 2017 alone. These attacks took place predominantly in Afghanistan and Pakistan and killed 1,018 people. The peace that accompanied the original Taliban occupation in the late 1990s was short-lived. Now, NATO and Western allies remain crucial supports to the Afghan government and military. Neither the government nor military is strong enough to withstand pressure from extremists without international support.

Understanding Afghanistan's Allies

Forces supplied by the United Nations under the direction of NATO have been holding the Taliban at bay and acting as a security force in the country since 2003–2004. The initial agreement was for ten years and was set to end in 2014. Known as the International Security Assistance Force (ISAF), these troops bolstered the current government and Afghan military to help them remain the controlling power in Afghanistan, but more needed to be done.

In January of 2015, NATO began a mission known as Resolute Support Mission (RSM). Unlike previous missions, the goal of this plan was not to assist Afghan forces in holding control of the nation. Instead, RSM's aim was to train Afghan security forces so that these internal forces were prepared to maintain control without external support. This plan was renewed in 2016, and RSM presence was increased from thirteen thousand troops to sixteen thousand troops in 2017. There are also plans to extend financial support into 2020. It is undeniable that true change for Afghanistan will come only when the nation is self-reliant. Only time will tell if RSM will provide the skills and resources necessary to reach this goal.

Over the Border

According to Dr. William Maley, one of the leading authorities on modern-day Afghanistan, Pakistan plays an important role in defeating the Taliban. The unsecured border between the two nations allows weapons and other material support for the Taliban to flow into and from Afghanistan unchecked. The weak border (and the lack of a Pakistani effort to secure it) allows freedom of movement for insurgents and for organizations like Pakistani Taliban to remain strong allies of the Afghan Taliban.

That is why air strikes, the American method for combating terrorism in the region, have had little effect on the Taliban. Air strikes targeted key players in the Afghan Taliban and were designed to force the Taliban to begin negotiating, but they did not disrupt the Taliban, because the power and ideology are not invested only in one person. The case of Mullah Omar is a good example of how the Taliban handled the strategy. When Omar died in 2013, the Taliban simply kept his death a secret until 2015. When his death was discovered, a new leader was chosen: Mullah Akhtar Mansour. Mansour was killed in a 2016 air strike. Once again, the Taliban named a successor. To the Taliban, the named leader of the organization is of little consequence. There will always be someone new to fill the role. Furthermore, the true power of the organization stems from their funding. Heroin and other narcotics are the lifeblood of the Taliban, and Pakistan will need to take a more proactive stance for real change to occur.

As long as Pakistan supports or at least does not truly impede the Taliban, other attempts to stop the insurgents' spread can seem futile. Drugs moving through the border between Pakistan and Afghanistan provide a huge portion of the Taliban's income on both sides of the border. That said, Pakistani support can also seem inexplicable. However, according to author and historian Joseph Micallef, a big motivator for continued Pakistani support of the Taliban could lie in the Durand Line. The Durand Line is an agreement between Afghanistan and Pakistan that increased the holdings of Pakistan by drawing land from Afghanistan. Through the Durand Line agreement, Pakistan maintains control of the following regions: the Swat Valley, Chitral, and Chageh. Should Afghanistan stabilize, Pakistan stands to lose those regions. Afghanistan could easily demand or simply take the land back.

While combating the Taliban, Afghanistan is in no position to contest ownership of the lands, and Pakistan directly benefits because the lands remain part of their country. To truly stabilize the nation, Afghanistan needs a stable border, and to have a stable border, Afghanistan needs Pakistani support. By closing the border, or even just tightening it, the Taliban loses their trade route for drug smuggling. With narcotics trade routes shut down, the terror organization could potentially lose power quickly because they would lose a major funding source.

Borders play another major role in the conflict. The rise of the Islamic State in the Middle East is fueling further violence in the region, and potential for collaboration between the two entities is an ever-looming threat. In August of 2017, that threat became apparent when ISIS and the Taliban coordinated a terror attack. Together, they killed fifty people in northern Afghanistan. The two organizations are battling one another for control of eastern Afghanistan, but collaboration in the north could continue to be problematic. The coordination of these terrorist groups could have terrible consequences in Afghanistan—and in the rest of the world. General John Nicholson, a commander of NATO and American forces in Afghanistan, says, "One of the things we are concerned about here in Afghanistan, the reason that the entire world needs to be focused on Afghanistan, is the potential for convergence among the various terrorist groups in this area." With the rising strength of ISIS and the increased Taliban resurgence, such a union remains a pressing threat.

Stopping the Opium Trade

Poppies in Helman province fuel the opium trade which helps fund Taliban efforts.

The greatest source of funds for the Taliban has been boosted by the group's control of Helmand, Afghanistan, which produces 80 percent of the opium poppies grown in the country. Afghanistan is currently the world's largest producer of opium. Increasing production generates important income. With this added income, the Taliban can continue to grow larger. The terror group has begun processing opium themselves, which has allowed them to produce more expensive products, such as morphine and heroin. These drugs are also easier to sell than the opium syrup that the Taliban originally dealt. In many ways, drugs are the lifeblood of the Taliban as an organization. Even the Afghan president, Ashraf Ghani, states that without the drug trade, the war "would have been long over."

Pakistani Resistance

Although the Pakistani government aids the Taliban, there are those in Pakistan who actively resist the ideals of the terror group. Gulalai Ismail is a Pakistani woman who, at the age of sixteen, decided to work toward a Pakistan that empowers girls and young women. Along with Saba Ismail, who was fifteen at the time, Jana Sana (then seventeen), and Sidra Jahangir (also seventeen), Ismail formed an organization focused on teaching girls about fundamental human rights. Aware Girls was born. The female-run organization operates in Pakistan and promotes gender equality, female empowerment, and peacemaking in the country. According to the organization, "the mission of Aware Girls is to empower young women, advocate for equal rights for young women, and to strengthen their capacity enabling them to act as agents of women empowerment and social change."

Men and women from many different regions in Pakistan, as well as Afghanistan, collaborate with Aware Girls. At a secret meeting in Peshawar in 2015, participants discussed strategies they'd used to fulfill the Aware Girls's mission. One man managed to convince shopkeepers not to sell guns to children. A woman who fought for the right to dress more freely succeeded in getting permission for women to wear colorful headscarves on a university campus. These are small, important victories for the group of three hundred activists, and significant progress toward the organization's larger goals.

The founders of Aware Girls advocate for education as a means to stop terrorism. Activists also campaign to stop violence against women including domestic abuse, acid attacks, exploitation, and murders like honor killings. Part of how they do this is by leading female groups to polling stations to ensure they can vote "freely and without intimidation." The members of Aware Girls are trying to give hope to a populace that has been ravaged by violence and war. Ismail conducts research on the psychological effects of terror on the people they are trying to aid, to increase Aware Girls's impact.

Other young people have joined them in their quest to bring peace. Jawad Ullah Khan was nineteen years old when he joined Aware Girls. He has seen atrocities carried out by the Taliban, such as a decapitated corpse left for the public to see, but he has found ways to work against the spread of such horrors. Ullah Khan has started a group of fifteen people within Aware Girls that reaches out to vulnerable young people in extremist madrasas through theater. His project works within the organization's goal of supporting vulnerable youth. Ullah Khan has found a way to connect with young people in schools and mosques to prevent terrorist recruitment.

The efforts of Aware Girls have helped increase access to health care, especially relating to the treatment of HIV and AIDS. They also now offer grants to small businesses owned by women with disabilities. As a whole, Aware Girls is an empowerment group giving women agency and freedoms in a traditionally male culture.

Changes Since 2001

Despite complex challenges, there has been movement forward in Afghanistan since the Taliban was removed from power in 2001. The greatest strides have been made in education. In 2001, there was no formalized education for girls at all to be found. Of all the male children, only one million were enrolled and attending school. By 2012, there were 7.8 million children enrolled, with a sizable portion of that number being girls.

There are other signs of progress as well. Women are returning to work and are taking positions in government. Though the people still fight for human rights and women's rights specifically, in 2014, 28 percent of the seats in the House of the People and the House of Elders in the Afghani government were occupied by women. These women work and fight hard to protect the interests of the people of Afghanistan. The voice of women in politics is an important step forward. Fawzia Koofi is a great example of a woman

FIGHTING TERROR ONLINE

Social media is the latest tool used by terrorist organizations, but social media platforms are fighting back. Between July 1 and December 31, 2015, nearly 380,000 accounts were suspended for promoting and supporting terrorism. Between August 1, 2015, and December 31, 2016, Twitter suspended 636,248 accounts that were affiliated with threats of terror or terror-related topics. Twitter has spoken out against the use of Twitter as a means of promoting terrorist ideology and has vowed to commit "to eliminating the promotion of violence and terrorism on our platform."

The convenience and ease of social media allow terror organizations to spread their messages far and wide, but the state department is looking for ways to stop the transmission of these posts. The US Department of State called for a meeting of the ministers of the Global Coalition on the Defeat of ISIS on March 22, 2017, in part to discuss the online presence of terror organizations and how to end their digital impact. Furthermore, the Global Counter ISIS Coalition Communications Working Group meets regularly with media and technology companies to discuss ways to counter terrorism online.

making her voice heard. Koofi is a member of parliament who fights diligently for the rights of women. One of her greatest triumphs thus far was the passage of the Elimination of Violence Against Women law in 2009. It outlaws the harassment of women on the street and in the work force.

People like Koofi do not get elected in a country without a will to change and move forward. The Afghani people are not giving up on their freedoms or their rights. In the face of more than three decades of atrocity after atrocity, injustice after injustice, they are still fighting for peace and independence. Though there are still great strides to be made and many injustices to be righted, Afghanistan is a country that refuses to give up on itself.

Teens Fighting Terror

More than half of the world's population is under the age of thirty. That is a large number of people that, if mobilized, could accomplish an incredible amount of change. This does not mean going out and fighting terrorists; it means using bright ideas to solve problems and leveraging the voices of young people to fight for social change. Neil Ghosh is the founder of Youth Resound, an organization dedicated to giving young people a voice on the global stage so they can share their ideas on how to solve issues in social justice and combat extremism.

BOOKS UNDER BURKAS

Malalai Joya began her social justice career in a Pakistani refugee camp. She was only four days old when the Soviets invaded Afghanistan. Her father stayed to fight the Soviets, but her mother took her and her nine siblings to refugee camps, first in Iran and then in Pakistan. Through her mother was illiterate, it was in those camps that Joya learned to read and write. She began teaching while there, and her own mother was one of her pupils. When she was only sixteen years old, Joya was smuggled back into Afghanistan by the Organization of Promoting Afghan Women's Capabilities to set up a secret school for girls. Using the very burka that the Taliban forced her to wear against her wishes, she challenged their authority. Though Joya hated the burka because it symbolized oppression to her, she used it to smuggle books to the girls in the school.

Joya has also been the director of a medical clinic and orphanage for children. She has served in parliament and been ousted from her position for her radical denouncements of the warlords. Today, Joya is considered a wanted woman by these warlords. She has survived at least six different assassination attempts and has to keep bodyguards with her at all times. Joya lives in hiding and rarely sees her husband for fear that he would be killed to get to her. Yet Joya is a fierce woman, not stopped by threats. Her work will not be stopped.

Ghosh advocates for empowering young people to develop ideas that improve the world. Speaking out against atrocities and raising awareness about terror is a great way for teens to combat terrorism without ever leaving their homes. Being informed about topics related to social change is a simple but large step toward making a difference in the world. With modern access to the internet and social media, teens are well equipped to stay informed and advocate for social justice and human rights, and create the kind of world they want to live in.

Terrorists and extremist groups have a huge impact on global politics. Nations are unifying in attempts to stamp out terror while terror organizations only continue to spread and grow. Though the Taliban seemed to be unseated from power in Afghanistan, they have grown stronger in recent years and once again control or occupy a significant portion of the country. The Pakistani Taliban continues to occupy border lands and grows stronger as time goes by. Both groups are active and carry out terror attacks, but they are not impervious and are not surviving unopposed. Young voices are some of the most powerful opponents to the oppression and heinous acts of violence committed by these terrorist organizations.

CHRONOLOGY

1947   Pakistan becomes independent from India.

1973   A military coup overthrows the
Afghan government.

1979   The Soviets invade Afghanistan.

1980s Pakistan houses Afghan refugees.

1989   Soviet troops leave Afghanistan.

1992   The mujahideen overthrow the government;
warlords start a civil war for control over
Afghanistan.

1996   The capital city of Afghanistan, Kabul, falls to
the Taliban, and the Taliban takes control of the
country.

2001   Al-Qaeda attacks the United States; the Taliban
does not turn over al-Qaeda leader Osama bin
Laden, so the United States invades Afghanistan.

2002–2004
The Pakistani Taliban is recognized as an
independent organization.

2013   Mullah Omar, leader of the Taliban dies, but his
death is hidden until 2015.

GLOSSARY

baad A practice in parts of Afghanistan that involves marrying off a young girl to pay a blood debt earned by a family member.

burka A loose garment worn by some Muslim women that covers them from head to toe.

chador A large piece of cloth used to cover the head and body but that leaves the face uncovered.

deradicalization The process of rehabilitating someone after they've been recruited and brainwashed.

hadith Sayings of the Muslim prophet Muhammad that are used by Muslims for guidance and wisdom.

infrastructure The basic structures and buildings needed for a society to function well.

jihad Holy war, struggle, or fight against enemies of Islam.

landlocked Surrounded by land with no access to a coast or the sea.

madrasas Schools used for religious instruction in Afghanistan.

mahram A male relative who acts as a chaperone to women.

mujahid An Afghani freedom fighter.

mullah A person educated in Islamic theology and Islamic law.

Pakistani Taliban A terrorist organization in Pakistan, formerly known as the TTP.

Pashtuns Members of the Pashto-speaking ethnic group living in Afghanistan and Pakistan.

propaganda Biased information used to promote a political cause or point of view.

Quran The Muslim holy book.

RAWA Revolution Association of Women of Afghanistan, a political/social organization of Afghan women working for women's rights and democracy.

refugee A person forced to leave their country to escape war, persecution, or a natural disaster.

sharia law Islamic law based upon the Quran and the hadith.

FURTHER INFORMATION

Books

Ellis, Deborah. *Kids of Kabul: Living Bravely Through a Never-Ending War*. Toronto, ON: Groundwood Books, 2012.

Yousafzai, Malala, and Christine Lamb. *I Am Malala: The Girl Who Stood Up for Education and Was Shot by the Taliban*. London, UK: Weidenfeld and Nicolson, 2013.

Websites

Mapping the Taliban

http://www.pbs.org/wgbh/pages/frontline/talibanlines/map/

This interactive map shows different sects of the Afghanistan and Pakistani Taliban and identifies the leaders of the different militias and Taliban supporters.

USGS Interactive Map

https://afghanistan.cr.usgs.gov/oil-and-natural-gas

This interactive map shows the different resources in Afghanistan and was developed to show the oil and gas resources in the country.

The Warlords of Afghanistan

https://www.washingtonpost.com/apps/g/page/
world/the-warlords-of-afghanistan/967/

Each of the warlords that fought for control of Afghanistan
in the 1990s, which led to the Taliban's control, are listed
here with brief biographies.

Videos

"Inside the Mind of a Suicide Bomber"

http://www.cnn.com/videos/world/2012/09/28/
coren-afghan-suicide-bomber.cnn

CNN's Anna Coren speaks with an incarcerated
suicide bomber.

"Malala Yousafzai Nobel Peace Prize Speech"

https://www.youtube.com/watch?v=MOqIotJrFVM

Malala Yousafzai accepted the Nobel Peace Prize on
December 10, 2014, for her activism for women's education
in direct defiance of the Pakistani Taliban—and at an
immense personal cost.

BIBLIOGRAPHY

Abbas, Hassan. "A Profile of Tehrik-i-Taliban Pakistan." *CTC Sentinel*, vol. 1. no. 2. (January 2008): 1–4. https://www.belfercenter.org/publication/profile-tehrik-i-taliban-pakistan.

"About RAWA." Revolutionary Association of the Women of Afghanistan. Retrieved November 23, 2017. http://www.rawa.org/rama.html.

Azami, Dawood. "How the Taliban groom child suicide bombers." BBC World Service, December 15, 2014. http://www.bbc.com/news/world-asia-27250144.

Azamy, Hekmatullah. "It's Complicated: The Relationship Between Afghanistan, Pakistan, and the Taliban." *Foreign Policy*, March 2, 2015. http://foreignpolicy.com/2015/03/02/its-complicated-the-relationship-between-afghanistan-pakistan-and-the-taliban/.

Briggs, Billy. "The Peshawar women fighting the Taliban: 'We cannot trust anyone.'" *Guardian*, October 13, 2015. https://www.theguardian.com/cities/2015/oct/13/the-peshawar-women-fighting-the-taliban-we-cannot-trust-anyone.

Benard, Cheryl. *Veiled Courage: Inside the Afghan Women's Resistance*. New York: Broadway Books, 2002.

Bezhan, Frud. "Afghan Police: Children Kidnapped to be
    Suicide Bombers For Taliban." Radio Free Europe Radio
    Liberty, June 10, 2017. https://www.rferl.org/a/afghan-
    police-children-kidnapped-by-taliban-to-be-suicide-
    bombers/28606744.html.

Brumfield, Ben. "Who are the Pakistani Taliban?" CNN World,
    October 17, 2012. http://www.cnn.com/2012/10/17/world/
    asia/pakistan-taliban-profile/index.html.

Caulfield, Philip. "Young Afghan wife who had nose cut
    off by Taliban debuts newly reconstructed face." *Daily
    News*, February 26, 2013. http://www.nydailynews.com/
    news/national/mutilated-afghan-wife-debuts-new-nose-
    article-1.1273781.

Clark, James. "Propaganda video shows and emboldened
    Taliban convoy traveling through Afghanistan in broad
    daylight." *Business Insider,* October 7, 2017. http://www.
    businessinsider.com/taliban-propaganda-video-convoy-
    traveling-in-afghanistan-in-daylight-2017-10.

Gopal, Anand. *No Good Men Among the Living: America,
    the Taliban, and the War through Afghan Eyes.* New York:
    Henry Holt and Company, 2014.

Ghosh, Neil. "To Fight Terror We Must Give Youth a Seat at
    the Table." *Huffington Post*, retrieved November 24, 2017.
    https://www.huffingtonpost.com/neil-ghosh/to-fight-
    terror-we-must- g_b_13854548.html.

Karasapan, Omer. "Rehabilitating child soldiers in the
    Middle East." Brookings, January 17, 2017. https://www.
    brookings.edu/blog/future-development/2017/01/17/
    rehabilitating-child-soldiers-in-the-middle-east/.

Joya, Malalai. *A Woman Among Warlords: The Extraordinary
    Story of an Afghan Who Dared to Raise Her Voice*. New
    York: Scribner, 2011.

Latifa. *My Forbidden Face: Growing Up Under the Taliban: A
    Young Woman's Story*. Translated by Lisa Appignanesi.
    London, UK: Virago Press, 2002.

Latifi, Ali M, and Abdul Matin Amiri. "A boy's life in
    Afghanistan; Anti-Taliban fighter at 9, dead at 12." *Los
    Angeles Times*, February 3, 2016. http://www.latimes.
    com/world/asia/la-fg-afghanistan-boy-fighter-20160203-
    story.html.

MacKenzie, Jean. "Life Under the Taliban." PRI, August 7,
    2009. https://www.pri.org/stories/2009-08-07/life-
    under-taliban.

Maley, William. *The Afghanistan Wars*. 2nd ed. New York:
    Palgrave Macmillan, 2009.

Mashal, Mujib, Ahim Abed, and Najim Rahim. "Joint Taliban-
    ISIS Attack Kills Dozens, Afghan Officials Say." *New
    York Times*, August 6, 2017. https://www.nytimes.
    com/2017/08/06/world/asia/taliban-islamic-state-attack-
    afghanistan.html.

Micallef, Joseph V. "How the Taliban Gets Its Cash." *Huffinton Post*, retrieved November 19, 2017. https://www.huffingtonpost.com/joseph-v-micallef/how-the-taliban-gets- its_b_8551536.html.

_____. "Why Pakistan Supports the Taliban." Military.com, April 25, 2017. http://www.military.com/daily-news/2017/04/25/why-pakistan-supports-taliban.html.

Morris, David Z. "Taliban Launches Smartphone App to Recruit and Spread Propaganda." *Fortune*, April 3, 2016. http://fortune.com/2016/04/03/taliban-launches-smartphone-app/.

Mufti, Shahan. "Funding the Pakistani Taliban." *PRI*, August 7, 2009. https://www.pri.org/stories/2009-08-07/funding-pakistani-taliban.

Nebehay, Stephanie. "Afghanistan is world's worst place to be born: U.N." Reuters, November 20, 2009. https://www.reuters.com/article/us-afghanistan-children-un/afghanistan-is-worlds-worst-place-to-be-born-u-n-idUSTRE5AI4QC20091120.

Rashid, Ahmed. *Taliban: Militant Islam, Oil and Fundamentalism in Central Asia.* 2nd ed. New Haven: Yale University Press, 2010.

Reynolds, Emma. "I'm sorry, I wish I could have stopped this': Jihadi Jake's father's heartwrenching message to Australia." News.com.au, March 22, 2015. http://www.news.com.au/entertainment/tv/im-sorry-i-wish-i-could-have-stopped-this- jihadi-jakes-fathers-heartwrenching-message-to-australia/news-story/3e7c9bbc1045b895579 48129f1238900.

Saifi, Sophia and Greg Botelho. "In Pakistan school attack, Taliban terrorists kill 145, mostly children." CNN World, December 17, 2014. http://www.cnn.com/2014/12/16/world/asia/pakistan-peshawar-school-attack/index.html.

Smallman, Etan. "Meet the 'other Malalas'- the Nobel Peace Prize winner's friends now heading to Edinburgh University." *Telegraph*, April 18, 2017. http://www.telegraph.co.uk/women/life/meet-malalas-nobel-peace-prize-winners-friends-now-heading/.

Woody, Christopher. "Heroin is driving a sinister trend in Afghanistan." *Business Insider*, October 30, 2017. http://www.businessinsider.com/taliban-control-of-heroin-drug- production-trafficking-in-afghanistan-2017-10.

Zargar, Arshad R. "A passion for food brings hope for the future." CBS News, May 27, 2016. https://www.cbsnews.com/news/afghan-refugees-build-new-lives-new-delhi-india-with- food/.

INDEX

Page numbers in **boldface** are illustrations

Akhundzada, Mawlawi
    Haibatullah, 18, 100
al-Qaeda, 21-22, 32, 38, 45,
    66
Aware Girls, 93-95

baad, 77
bin Laden, Osama, 22, 45, 66
Bureau of Counterterrorism
    and Countering Violent
    Extremism, 16-17
burka, 7, 15, 24, **39**, 69, 74,
    98

Cable, Mullah, 47-49, 58
Chador, 24, 69
child soldiers, **46**, 50-58, **56**,
    61, 63
Cold War, 11-12, 29, 31
Communist, 11, 13, 30-32
coup, 10-11, 24, 27, 30

deradicalization, 53-54

drug/narcotics trade, 20, 28,
    44, 60, 83, 90-92, **92**

education, 10, 15, 35, 39–41,
    48, 50, 53–54, 67–69, 71,
    75, 78–82, 84, 94–95

Federally Administered Tribal
    Areas (FATA), 10, 38, 85

Global Counterterrorism
    Forum (GCTF), 16–17

hadith, 14
human rights, 22, 44, 53, 93,
    95, 99

infrastructure, 83
ISIS, 16, 91–92, 96

jihad, 48–50, 55, 61
Joya, Malalai, 98

Kabul, 11, 22, **26**, 35, 39, 43,
    43, **51**, 69, 72
kidnappings, 13, 20, 35, 47,
    54

landlocked, 9

madrasas, 50, **51**, 52, 54,
    60–61, 63, 94
mahram, 24
mujahideen, 12–13, 30–32, **57**
mullah, 6, 13, 18, 45, 47–49,
    58, 89–90

NATO (North Atlantic Treaty
    Organization), 7, 87–88,
    91

Omar, Mullah Mohammad, 13,
    13, 18, 45, 49, 89

Pakistani Taliban, 18–19,
    36–38, 40–41, 60, 65, 67,
    85, 89, 99
Pashtuns, 33–34, 57
propaganda, 50, 60–63, **62**

Quran, 14, 49, 51, 60, 81

ransom, 20
RAWA (Revolution
    Association of Women of
    Afghanistan), 22, 71–72,
    74–75, 78–79

recruitment, 50–54, 56–58, 61,
    63, 94
refugee, 5, 32, 36, 84
refugee camps, 5–6, 33, 98

secret schools, 71, 78–81, 98
September 11 attacks, 44–45,
    66
sharia law, 13–15, 18, 23–24,
    34–36, 38, 60, 77
Shia Muslim, 9
social media, 60–61, 82–83,
    96, 99
Soviet influence, 11–14, 23,
    25, 29–33, 35–37
suicide bomb, 48–50, 54,
    59–60, 63
Sunni Muslim, 9–10

United Nations, 42–44, 56–57,
    88

warlords, 12, 14, 21, 23, 28,
    32–34, 41, 48, 98
women's rights, 15, 22,
    29–30, 68–69, 71, 73, 75,
    93, 95, 97

Yousafzai, Malala, 40, 67–69,
    71

ABOUT THE AUTHOR

Cassandra Schumacher has a background in anthropology and creative writing. She is the author of *Code Breakers and Spies of the American Revolution* and the co-author of *Cultures of the World: Papua New Guinea.*